TEACH YOURSELF BOOKS

DRAWING

Some Other Teach Yourself Books

———

TEACH YOURSELF BOOKS

DRAWING

RONALD SMITH
A.T.D. (Lond.)

TEACH YOURSELF BOOKS
ST. PAUL'S HOUSE WARWICK LANE LONDON EC4

First printed 1942
This impression 1970

ISBN 0 340 05562 6

Printed in Great Britain for The English Universities Press Ltd.,
by Richard Clay (The Chaucer Press), Ltd., Bungay, Suffolk

PREFACE

In these days of widespread general education and of almost universal ability to read and write we are inclined to under-estimate the importance of drawing to the person who is not by training an artist. The average man, having a message to convey, quite naturally writes a letter; if he has a house to let he prints a notice to that effect; if a theory or teaching to study or expound, he resorts to books and pamphlets. Novels, circulars, tracts and newspapers crowd in upon our day, and we take them all very much for granted, thinking of them, if we think of them at all, as quite indispensable to us.

Not so long ago, however, things were quite different. A few highly educated men and women, chiefly priests and nobles, were able to read and write as we do but the great masses of people could be appealed to only by paintings, drawings and carvings. Even the spoken language used by the priests (Latin) was largely unintelligible to their flock, whose knowledge of the Bible story was derived almost entirely from such illustrative carvings as those on the walls and portals of Amiens cathedral. Cathedrals of this period are often referred to as the " Bible of the poor ".

Many of our own mediaeval churches are full of mural paintings conveying similar messages in clear, powerful drawing which we should all find an opportunity of studying. The lurid scenes of Judgment Day which appear in some of them could scarcely have failed to convert even the most hardened sinner.

Many of you will know, also, the poster which, much nearer to our own times, was exhibited to the aborigines and the early settlers in Australia. This, an announcement that blacks and whites would be subject to the same law and each equally liable to punishment by death for committing murder, took a form similar to the strip cartoon popular in our daily papers, and its message was understood, perfectly, by all.

Thus, drawing, which came hundreds of thousands of years before the written word, and from which, indeed, by way of pictographs and symbols, lettering itself gradually developed, is still the most universal language of all.

We know that, some twenty thousand years before Christ, the cave-dweller returning from his hunting would spend the dark hours painting and drawing on the rough walls of his home, helped perhaps by the flickering light from a fire. Intensely observed pictures of the animals he had slain and of those which had eluded him are still to be seen in parts of France and Spain.

We know, too, that there are among us today some who return home from very different work in city, factory or field, and find the same satisfaction and a great deal of healthy " release " in leisure hours spent with pencil and brush. Our mode of life has, in the course of these thousands of years, changed entirely; crude earth colours and bone palettes have given way to more satisfactory materials and we have behind us the accumulated knowledge and experiment of the ages, but, in his general attitude towards drawing and in his constant concern with it, man has, in fact, changed surprisingly little.

Palaeolithic and twentieth-century draughtsmen alike are moved by a desire to create—a need for self-expression which is almost as urgent as the need for food and drink.

Such drawing and painting may sometimes be instrumental in the provision of these other necessities, serving a purpose more serious even than the expression of the artists' *joie de vivre* and of his excited interest in the appearance of things about him. When fortune failed to smile upon our caveman in the chase, he would draw a bison in its death-struggle or place a well-painted spear in the vitals of an existing drawing to invoke the assistance of whatever gods he considered responsible for his success or failure.

In every age the arts have been turned to the service of religion, and in Europe, until the Reformation, the Christian Church was chief patron of them all. Since then that position has been held in turn by the State, the nobility, royalty, and, last century, by the new moneyed class which was produced by the Industrial Revolution and whose members saw in the possession of pictures and *objets d'art* a possible source of social prestige.

This century the patron *par excellence* of the arts is, of course, Industry, and most artists, whatever may be their private opinions and ambitions, turn for bread and butter, and not infrequently a little jam as well, to commercial art.

It may be that you, in turning to a book on drawing, have one eye on commercial art as a likely source of income; that, like your prehistoric ancestor, you are not entirely free from ulterior motives. On the other hand, you may wish to teach yourself to draw for purely cultural reasons, because you have a " feeling " for drawing and know what an absorbing pastime it can be. Whichever it may be, this book is designed to help you. You must not expect to learn from it all that there is to know about drawing. A whole lifetime of study and effort is scarcely sufficient to do that, and the greatest artists, the men of highest achievement and widest reputation, are most ready to admit that they still have much to learn and that they are, in fact, always students.

The book is intended, however, as a guide to such study and effort—a pointer towards the success which, assuming considerable application on your part, you may well attain.

Read the whole book carefully to begin with, then, returning to Chapter I or II and applying yourself seriously to the practical work suggested, you will see each stage of your progress in relation to the whole course, and you will know to which part of the book you must refer when particular difficulties arise.

R. S.

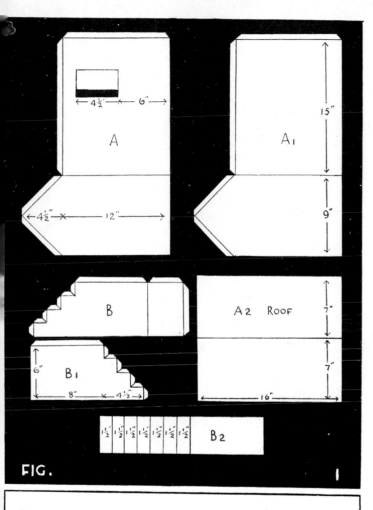

A

← 4½" → × ← 6" →

A₁

15"

9"

B

A₂ ROOF

7"

B₁

6"

← 8" → × ← 4½" →

7"

← 16" →

1½" 1½" 1½" 1½" 1½" 1½" 1½" B₂

FIG.

1

DIAGRAMS—**A** of the House, and **B** of the flight of steps in Plate 1. All the hinges are half an inch wide.

[To face page viii.

[*Photograph by J. V. Parry*

PLATE 1.

A GROUP OF CARDBOARD MODELS. Diagrams for making the house and the flight of steps will be found in Fig. 1. The tall chimney once contained a roll of linoleum and the fence is a piece of corrugated packing paper. Both were whitened with poster paint.

See Chapter V and the end of Chapter I.

CONTENTS

CHAPTER I

CHAPTER II

CHAPTER III

CONTENTS

CHAPTER X

LIST OF ILLUSTRATIONS

PLATES IN HALF-TONE

CHAPTER I

DRAWING MATERIALS

THE tools and materials necessary for teaching oneself to draw are few and inexpensive, clean in use and easily cared for. One of the chief recommendations of drawing as a home occupation is, indeed, the fact that most ambitious work can be done with the very minimum of expense and apparatus. It has been put on record that masterpieces have been made with charred matchsticks on scrap paper and, although I have never, myself, come across these, they may very well exist. I have seen wonderful drawings made with stubby little pencil-ends which most people would have thrown away long since, while, to judge from their work in the Museums, our Old Masters had a special weakness for sugar-bags and writing-paper.

Simplicity and economy in materials are, as a matter of fact, conducive to like qualities in one's work, and these are among the hall-marks of the artist. Certain it is, anyway, that you should avoid too great a concern with your materials, for they can easily become a mania. Buy the necessary things only, buy the very best, and then use them. Some amateurs buy ostentatious outfits full of pretty but useless gadgets, and become so deeply engrossed with them that they never get down to any real work at all.

I shall deal in this chapter with those materials which are really essential.

1. The Pencil.

The pencil is the most necessary of all materials, and perhaps the least considered. I wonder how many artists ever pause to reflect upon its perfection.

The lead of the pencil is made from a mixture of plastic clay and graphite or plumbago. This mixture in paste form is put into a large metal cylinder having a plunger at one end and a perforated plate at the other.

The plunger forces the paste through the holes in the plate as thin rods, which, broken off to pencil length, are dried and fired to red heat. These are then encased in cedar-wood by a very ingenious process.

A paste containing one-tenth clay and the rest graphite produces a pencil of medium hardness, known as the HB (Hard Black). If the proportion of graphite in the paste is increased, softer and blacker pencils are produced, B, 2B, 3B. If the proportion of clay is increased the pencil becomes harder, F (firm), H, 2H, 3H.

It is possible to obtain pencils as hard as 6H and as soft as 6B and, of course, all intermediate degrees, but those beyond H are intended for precision work, and are too hard for our purpose, while those softer than 2B tend to get out of hand. You will learn from experience which degree suits you best and then, for all ordinary purposes, you will stick to it. It may be necessary sometimes, in the same drawing, to use more than one degree of pencil, but you will find yourself doing so less as you discover other, more laudable, ways of bringing variety into your work. You may find a slight variation in the degrees of different makers; the H of one may be equivalent to the HB of another, but here again experience will be your guide.

After many trials I now use a Royal Sovereign HB pencil. It is very sympathetic and has a very wide range indeed, so that I seldom need turn to the H or the B. It costs fourpence, which is the average price for a pencil of good quality.

Your pencil, when you have it, should be treated carefully, for if it is dropped, the lead inside may break into short lengths and fall out when the pencil is sharpened. It is as well, also, to protect the sharpened point with a tin cap, particularly if the pencil is to be carried in the pocket.

Few people sharpen a pencil to the best advantage; too many cut away more than they use. To begin with you should make sure that you are sharpening the pencil at the end opposite to the letters which denote the degree. If these are cut away the pencil will lose its identity. You should then hold the pencil securely in the left hand, its end resting along the fleshy part of the thumb. Then make your first cut. The bent first finger of the right hand supplies the power behind the knife and the left thumb is supported by the right (Fig. 2).

The cut should begin rather less than an inch along the pencil and sweep right down to the end, not exposing the lead. The pencil is turned a little and a second cut made, then a third and a fourth until the first cut reappears. This process is repeated until the lead is gradually exposed. This will come to a point quite

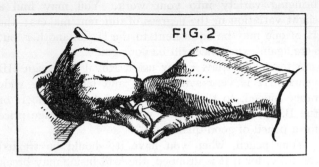

FIG. 2

naturally with the cutting of the wood, and should appear as in Fig. 3A, not as in B.

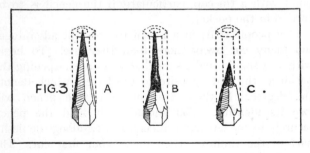

FIG.3   A   B   C .

Notice that the point of the sharpened pencil should, ideally, have been right at the end of the original uncut lead (Fig. 3A).

Sharpening such as that in Fig. 3C is most wasteful; the lead cut away there would have been sufficient to make a whole drawing.

There are other ways of sharpening a pencil, of course, and in the hands of those who are used to them, they may be just as effective. The method I am advocating is better than the more usual one of holding the pencil in mid air and sharpening it away from the body because here, with no cushion-like thumb for support, the point is subjected to a strong downward pressure from the knife at the end of every cut, and it tends to snap off.

Copying pencils in which dye replaces the graphite should never be used for drawing.

2. The Knife.

An ordinary pen-knife is as good as anything. It is false economy to buy any but the very best, for a soft steel retains its sharpness only for a very short time. Your knife need not be very large, but it should always be razor sharp. If you adopt my method of pencil-sharpening you will need a pen-knife, for no other kind is really suitable, and if it is as sharp as I suggest, you will have to be careful not to cut your thumb.

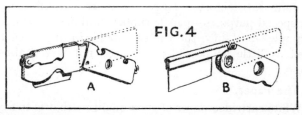

FIG. 4

A   B

Very popular among draughtsmen and students now is the razor-blade. It is useful for cutting mounts and a host of other jobs, and if you sharpen your pencils away from the body it can be used for that too, although, for obvious reasons, it cannot be used for the other and better method. It should be used in a holder specially designed for the purpose, called a Jigger Knife. Figs. 4A and B show holders for the double and single edged blades respectively. Pencil sharpeners are, to my mind, unsatisfactory.

The pencil must never be allowed to get blunt, so the knife should be always at hand. Some people use a small block covered with sandpaper—a matchbox does excellently—and keep their pencils pointed on this.

3. The Rubber.

This should be fairly soft and must be kept very clean. It should be rubbed on a scrap of paper or on the edge of your drawing just before it is actually used, or a greasy smudge which is quite ineradicable may result. It should not be held in the hand while drawing, for the least drop of perspiration will render it useless.

When it is new you may find it to be covered with a white powder or gummy substance. This should all be scraped off before it is used. The ordinary India rubber is quite satisfactory. There are other varieties, used for special purposes—plastic rubbers and art erasers, for example—but since the rubber should, in any case, be used as little as possible, you need not worry about these.

4. The Paper.

White cartridge paper of good quality—that is to say, as white and heavy as possible—provides the best surface on which to draw. It should be purchased in Imperial sheets ($22'' \times 30''$) and cut into two or four as required. It has the advantage of being quite inexpensive.

At all costs you should avoid drawing-blocks, especially if you intend using a wash of colour, for they cockle in a most unpleasant fashion.

Good cartridge paper will take a wash quite well, especially if it is stretched before use.

To do this you should damp the paper thoroughly on one side, paste the edges to a depth of about half an inch on that side, and lay it, damp side downwards, on a large drawing-board. See that the edges stick thoroughly and, if necessary, apply gummed paper tape along them. As the paper dries it will tighten up like a drum.

Some people do this as a preparation for pencil drawing as well, but I should not advise it. For colour-work and wash-drawing it is necessary and, if you are using Whatman or any of the other special, thick water-colour papers, it is essential, but for ordinary drawing, a board and some drawing-pins—or " thumb-tacks "— will be quite adequate.

For outdoor work a sketch-book seems suitable, but I have certain rooted objections to them; for one thing, they are very uncomfortable in use, especially the larger ones. It is better to carry loose sheets of paper in a stiff portfolio which can in turn be used as a drawing-board. Specially designed cases for this purpose are sold, with clips to hold your drawing on the outside ; but something of the sort can be made very easily at home.

5. The Drawing-board.

This at its simplest may be a very stout piece of strawboard; at its best, battened behind with mahogany, keyed and proof against warping, shrinking and all other dangers, it may cost several pounds. Most satisfactory for our purpose is a deal board clamped at each end like a pastry-board, or a piece of thick plywood which needs no battening and costs about five shillings in the half-Imperial size and a little more for the Royal.

An accurate foot ruler will be useful, and also a plumb-line.

6. Pens.

Pens will not be necessary until you reach Chapter VIII. For these you could not do better than obtain catalogues of William Mitchell's Gillotts and Perry pens. You will find in them everything that you will be likely to need and a great deal to interest you. For pen-drawing you may require several different kinds of nibs, but one fine, flexible kind in combination with brush-work can be made to do almost anything.

7. Brushes.

These, like pencils and knives, need to be as good as money can buy. Cheap brushes wear out very quickly and they are never satisfactory in use.

A brush should be springy. The hairs, when bent back and released, should spring into their original position. They should also take a point quite readily when the brush is wetted thoroughly and shaken. Sable brushes meet these requirements better than any.

One good-sized sable, about as thick as a pencil and long in proportion, will do to begin with, giving broad washes and fine lines equally well. You can add other sizes and kinds as new needs arise.

These, for the moment, are all the materials I am going to discuss. Certain others will claim your attention when we get to Chapter VIII, but, for the moment, remember—choose few, but choose carefully!

The next few chapters of this book deal with the drawing of solid objects indoors, and for your first subjects I want you to have a few models of such things as cubes, cylinders, chimneys, houses, and flights of steps—all made of white cardboard. I want you to make these models yourself. You will gain, in making them, an understanding of construction and form, and a feeling for the solidity of things which will materially assist your drawing later.

Fig. 1 gives you working measurements for the construction of the objects in Plate I. All that you will require to make them is some fairly thin, easily bent, white cardboard, your knife, a pencil, a ruler and, to join the parts together, a pot of Gloy or a tin of Gripfix.

It is important that the cardboard should be white and without gloss, for the models will be used in studying shade and shadows and the varying degrees of darkness in them—things most clearly seen where there is neither colour nor reflection to complicate them.

These models used for drawing have certain advantages over other objects. Their whiteness and consequent susceptibility to subtle light and shade is one. A very few of them can be arranged in an infinite number of ways, so that there need be no monotony. They are basic in form. Cylinders, cubes, spheres and cones occur in all natural objects: the great French painter Cézanne showed that everything can be painted in terms of them. They must be thoroughly understood before other, more complex things—trees, people or animals— can be drawn well.

The houses, chimneys and simple architectural objects are particularly useful again later on, when similar real architecture is to be drawn or painted. Many old masters, including painters of the wonderful Italian Renaissance, painted their buildings from such models, arranged in the lighting they required.

You should also begin collecting together, quite soon, any other natural or fashioned objects which, because of their form or texture, interest you—shells, fir-cones, bones, jars, even stones of unusual shape. A number of these should be white also, for reasons which I have already explained.

You will see that I have made no mention here of flat " copies ", and, if you have been in the habit of using any such things—pictures, postcards or draw- ings—I want you to stop doing so at once. It is essen- tial to see for oneself at first hand; and in future you should draw from real, solid things, and from these alone.

PLATE 2.

A Pencil Drawing (5¾″ × 7½″) reproduced by the half-tone process.
(*See* Chapter X, page 169). It is one of several studies made for an
illustration and some colour which seemed likely to be of use has
been suggested (*see* Chapter X, page 173—Representation of Colour).

[*To face page 24.*

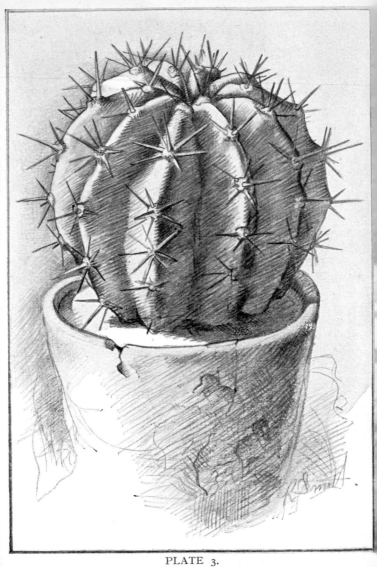

PLATE 3.

CACTUS : a pencil drawing reproduced actual size by the half-tone
process. (*See* Chapter X, page 169.) Light and shade have been
used here to express form only. No attempt has been made to
suggest colour. (*See* Chapter II—The Intention of Your Drawing.)

CHAPTER II

OBJECT DRAWING—BEGINNING

Preliminary Arrangements.

HAVING all the materials necessary for your drawing, and having laid somewhere on one side the various objects which you have made and collected, you should now select a room in which to work. If possible, find one with north windows, which receives no direct sunshine at any time of the day, and arrange yourself so that the light falls on your paper from the left-hand side. If you are left-handed it should come, of course, from the right-hand side. This is important, because the shadow of your drawing hand must not fall across your work.

One can work standing or sitting, according to preference. The Art School " donkey " (Fig. 5A) is comfortable, if you desire to sit. It gives a convenient rest for the drawing-board and allows you to slide back and view your work from a distance, without actually rising. A simple alternative to this consists of two chairs tied together by the front legs (Fig. 5B).

You must also get hold of a small table, a little over thirty inches in height, on which to arrange your group. This should be set squarely in front of you and be seen directly over the drawing-board, which should rest on your knees and be at right angles to your " line of sight ". Fig. 6A is the plan of a draughtsman sitting in such correct relation with his board and group, while Fig. 6B shows a not uncommon and quite incorrect arrangement. If you wish to stand, an easel is necessary, and if, later on, you decide to do some oil painting, it will be found absolutely essential. Winsor & Newton's Radial Easel is excellent. It is firm and thoroughly practical and quite inexpensive. It should be placed to the right or left of the line of sight, according to whether you are right- or left-handed. Your subject is seen thus, beside the drawing-board, and neither is obscured by your raised arm (Fig. 6c).

Drawings made sitting and standing differ somewhat in character. The latter have, as a rule, greater freedom and verve, and give the impression of having come from the shoulder rather than from the wrist. The whole arm is in action when you stand at an easel, and it is difficult not to be bold and direct.

The former, demanding none of the real physical effort involved in making an easel drawing, lend themselves to closer and more prolonged study, and tend, therefore, to be more disciplined and complete.

It is, in my opinion, better to sit, at any rate for your early drawings.

Whichever you eventually decide to do, you will almost certainly need to readjust your pencil-hold. The usual way of holding it between your thumb and the first and second fingers, so that it points over your shoulder, is a writing method. Movement is made at the wrist and is continually restricted. For drawing you should get into the habit of holding your pencil as shown in Fig. 8, with all four fingers beneath it,

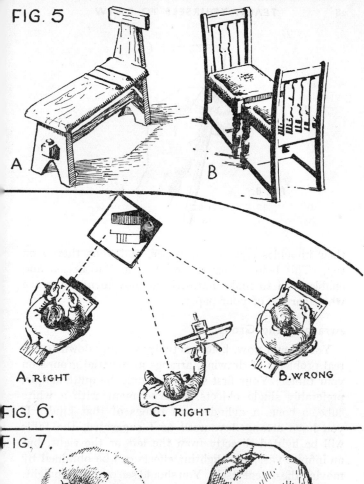

FIG. 5

A

B

FIG. 6.

A. RIGHT

C. RIGHT

B. WRONG

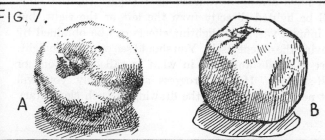

FIG. 7.

A

B

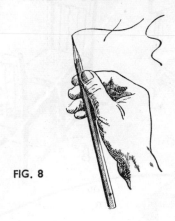

FIG. 8

their knuckles against the paper, and your thumb on top. This hold brings the whole arm into action and enables you to make unrestricted movements over the whole surface of your paper.

Arranging the Group.

You should now, before actually settling down to the real problems of drawing, arrange a few trial groups on your table. Your first subjects should be quite simple, preferably single objects, so experiment with a white cube, a cone, a cylinder and things of that kind. If you have arranged yourself as I suggested, the table will be lighted directly from the left or the right, but an infinite variety of lighting effects can be obtained by moving the object itself. You should see part of it in light, part in shade and part in what is called half-tone or half-shadow. If you progress satisfactorily you will not need to linger over the drawing of such elementary objects, so try arranging some rather more ambitious groups.

If you have found a few objects which for some reason really excite you, try, now, to arrange them in a lively way, stressing that aspect of them which first attracted you.

You may sometimes be very exact in your arrangements, keeping the objects in their true context, avoiding any incongruity. If, for example, you decide to draw a dog's water-bowl, you will draw it from above, as you normally see it. With it will be a couple of dog biscuits or a slipper, which you might well expect to find near by. A hall lantern would be drawn from below, a Chelsea porcelain figure, pipe and tobacco pouch, at your eye level, as though they lay on a mantelself, and so on.

At other times, to avoid monotony, you might deliberately seek incongruity in your grouping. The Surrealist painters give us such fantastic combinations as a lobster reclining on a bowler hat, or the plaster cast of an eye in a bird cage, which are very good fun and no less useful as exercises than more prosaic groups.

The objects in any group need not be symmetrical, but they should be balanced. If, for example, you have a tall object—say, a bottle—and two others, one large and one small, the large object could be placed near to the bottle on one side and the small one farther away on the other side, and a balance be effected.

It is almost essential to have some strong vertical interest in a group or picture, and also something horizontal. This gives stability. For the same reason, curves and rounded forms should always be accompanied by straight lines and flat surfaces.

It is possible, of course, with experience, to put into a drawing or painting, balance, stability and qualities of design which do not actually exist in the subject or group. Do not attempt to show the whole of each of your objects, separating them entirely one from another. Some of them are sure to be obscured in part by others, if the arrangement is to appear natural.

Always be on the look-out for ready-made subjects— on your dressing-table, in the scullery or outhouse: things falling accidentally into groups which conscious arrangement could never rival. Draw them *in situ* if conditions are not too bad or reconstruct them in your " studio ".

But we must return a little.

The Intention of Your Drawing.

Having your first simple subject arranged and your materials to hand, it is essential to get a clear understanding of what you are attempting to do. The student tackles such work as this, to obtain knowledge to master the craft and science of drawing. He is not concerned here with beauty or art, any more than is the child who hammers out scales on the piano, but he is acquiring the stuff from which such things are made.

Beauty, indeed, has a habit of creeping in unexpectedly and uninvited. Great artists whose work is praised for its qualities of expression or mood have often produced these qualities quite unconsciously, while, consciously, they wrestled with some technical idea.

First of all you must realise that to draw a thing is to reconstruct it as we understand and see it from one fixed point of view. Such reconstruction demands, of course, a careful analysis of the appearance of the object, and great concentration. Absent-minded copying is not at all the same thing.

Again, drawing has certain obvious limitations. You cannot, for example, represent colour with a black lead pencil, and no attempt should be made to do so. Local colour, where it occurs, must be ignored. Everything must be treated as though it were white. The brown of a teapot contrasted with the whiteness of the table-cloth, and the black of hair or eyebrows against the pale colour of a face, find no expression in drawing. We are concerned with these things purely as solids. It is their form which we must reconstruct, showing, on our drawing-paper, that they are rounded and smooth or sharp of edge and composed of flat surfaces; that one thing is near to us, the next farther away.

We are concerned, too, with the essential form of things—with a cube as a cube, not as a wooden object which is dented here and there and splintered at the edges. We must avoid sentimentality and that love of the picturesque which breaks every fence, cracks every wall, and paints moss on every crumbling roof. Such things have their place, but it is not here. We must ignore, in short, the superficial things for the more important underlying ones. The solid, bony structure of a cow is more important than its furry appearance, the general direction and undulation of ground more important than the grass and weeds growing on it.

Our aim is, then, to create an illusion of solidity, an

effect of depth and space on our paper; it is, as Seurat, the French painter, said, to " hollow out the picture space ".

We are made aware of depth and of the form of things about us, partly by light and by the shades and shadows consequent upon it, partly by the direction and apparent length of the lines bounding and composing these things. These factors must be well understood if we are to create the necessary illusion. Each has been thoroughly analysed, and we have a guide to our own research in " Light and Shade " and in " Perspective " or fore-shortening which will be dealt with in detail in subsequent chapters.

These sciences are, however, the outcome of careful observation, and for the time being you will do well to train your own powers in that direction. Rules can be really useful only when the need for them has been felt.

The Drawing.

Don't push your drawing away into one corner of the paper. You should aim at placing it centrally— with an equal space at the sides and top and a slightly deeper space below.

If you replaced your board with a sheet of glass and, looking through it at the model, you traced an outline with chalk or crayon, you would obtain a sight-size drawing. The nearer the board or glass to the model, the larger this drawing would be, and vice versa. Unless there is some good reason for not doing so, you should make your drawings sight size. Otherwise you will be mentally enlarging or reducing what you see, and causing yourself unnecessary work.

Holding your pencil in the correct and easy way, you should indicate the size and position of your object or objects very lightly indeed. These marks will almost certainly need correction and, since use of the rubber is to be avoided as much as possible, they should be only just visible, so loose and non-committal that they can be adjusted and then ignored. Don't hesitate to make such second shots. The existence of two or more lines—one right, the others wrong, indicates growth in your drawing and shows that it has life. This is infinitely more important than mere " finish ". Be quite certain that neatness, just as such, is of no value at all in drawing. It is not by accident that some work is described as " dead right."

You should watch carefully the apparent direction and length of these main lines. Compare their inclination with the horizontal and vertical—*e.g.*, with your pencil held out horizontally and with a plumb-line. The pencil held out at arm's length can also be used to measure the relative length of foreshortened lines, if its distance from your eye be kept constant. Such mechanical aids are really helpful at first, but they will be discarded, and rightly so, as your eye itself gains in judgment.

You will find it useful to compare and adjust certain obvious shapes in subject and drawing—the triangle formed by three important points, for example—the contour of the whole group or the angles between important lines in different objects.

While you are doing this you should be observing, and showing in your drawing, which parts of your group or object are in light and which dark. Decide which of the dark areas is darkest of all, which next and so on; which of the light parts is lightest of all. See if in any part there is a gradual change from light to dark; if any dark plane looks particularly dark where it comes in contact with a light plane. Consider the background too. Does it seem to be equally light or dark all over, or does it appear to vary, affected by the proximity of the lights and darks of the group? Does it emphasise or soften the edges of any of the objects? *Have in mind always the form of the object*, and see that your shading is really expressing that form. Reason out anything which seems to you strange or contradictory here. It is no use merely copying shading.

It is usual to shade everything, no matter what direction the form takes, in roughly parallel lines, which in the case of a right-handed man will go from top right to bottom left. This allows very subtle gradations and changes of tone, and the movement from wrist, elbow or shoulder is very natural.

You can, however, shade left-handed, in dots or in scribbles; any one way is as good as any other.

Notice the shadows cast on the background and on the table. Study their boundaries just as you do the boundaries of the objects themselves. See how they compare for darkness with the shade on the objects.

There should be no clear-cut distinction between this shading and your outlining. The two are interdependent and should be used concurrently. Begin sometimes with the shading, introducing outline only when really necessary, perhaps not at all (Fig. 7A). Remember that outline is only a convention, and that, used indiscreetly, it can do more harm than good, actually destroying a sense of solidity (Fig. 7B).

Finally compare subject and drawing carefully and see how the two still differ. Learn all you can from the comparison. Make several such drawings, arranging your subjects so that they increase in difficulty— e.g., a cube first, then boxes with lids open, then cardboard models and similar angular objects; then introduce objects with curves, still all preferably white, and see how you get on with drawing ellipses. The other bits and pieces you have collected and some of your trial groups will provide further models at this stage. Some of them will be, I expect, bright in hue, and will give you practice in ignoring colour while you search for form.

When you feel that you have done enough of this, you should turn to the succeeding chapters III and IV, and master their contents. Have a pencil and paper by your side and translate the text into diagrams as you read, puzzling out graphically any points which you find difficult. This done, return to your objects and groups and draw several more of them, applying your new knowledge.

You will find yourself drawing more slowly, because you are getting more out of your subject, because you are seeing more in it. Your reconstructing will be based on a firmer understanding of construction, your observation will be more systematic—you will know what to look for in the subject, what you can expect to find.

Chapter V will take you stage by stage through such an advanced drawing, and, beyond that, we shall break new ground.

FIG. 9.

CHAPTER III

PERSPECTIVE

THERE are two kinds of perspective—aerial and linear. Aerial perspective is concerned with the tone and colour of objects, with their relative distinctness and the effect of atmosphere upon their appearance. Linear perspective, as its name suggests, deals with the linear aspect of things and enables one to reproduce accurately, on a flat surface, the form, outline, relative position and magnitude of objects as they appear to the eye. It is this linear aspect with which we are concerned here.

Its Origin.

There have been, of course, countless great periods of Art in which nothing was known of perspective. The caveman of our preface and the Egyptians later were not concerned at all, in their painting, with questions of depth or solidity; neither were the artists of Persia,

Japan or Byzantium, nor the artist craftsmen of the Middle Ages. Not indeed until the fourteenth century was there any real concern with the third dimension in picture-making.

Just before that time a renaissance or rebirth of learning had come to Italy, and with it a burst of great activity in the arts and, in Florence particularly, a restless curiosity which sought to analyse and explain everything in terms of science. Such curiosity was frowned upon by the Church, however, and many of these Florentines who might well have become great scientists, turned instead to painting. It is not surprising, therefore, that the visual aspect of things came in for so large a share of question and experiment.

A clearly scientific spirit is revealed in the works of Uccello, Signorelli, Piero della Francesca and a score of others, while that versatile genius Leonardo da Vinci has left a treatise on painting which deals with little else but anatomy, light and shade and perspective.

The Perspective Apparatus.

You will already have discovered, in your drawing, that the actual shape of an object is very different from its apparent shape. All the angles of a square are right angles, but, when it is drawn foreshortened, its angles are all different, and none of them is a right angle. Beginners find great difficulty in getting used to this, tending always to draw the true shape instead of the apparent shape.

One draughtsman, centuries ago, overcame this difficulty by constructing a drawing-machine (Fig. 9). It consisted of a vertical sheet of glass erected on a table-top, with a fixed peep-hole some distance away from the glass and above the base. One eye was applied to the peep-hole so that it looked along a line perpendicular to the glass (the direction-of-sight line); the other eye would be closed. An object placed in any position behind the glass could be seen through it and traced in outline on to it. This tracing would be a true representation of the object as it appeared to the eye at that fixed point.

To understand this one must remember that the object is made visible by the light shining on it. An infinite number of rays of light illuminate the object and are reflected from it, in straight lines, in all directions. One set of these reflected rays converges on to the eye and conveys to it an image of the object.

The sheet of glass intercepts these visual rays, and each passes through it in a point. These points are plotted and joined up when the tracing is made, forming another exact image whose size increases or decreases as the glass is brought nearer to the object or the eye (Fig. 10).

When, with one eye shut, you extend a pencil to determine the apparent length of a foreshortened line, you are, in effect, measuring the distance between two rays as they pass through an imaginary plane which is at right angles to your direction-of-sight line and at arm's length from your eye.

Study of tracings made on glass showed that the apparent shape of an object is subject to certain invariable laws which, if there is sufficient data, enable one to reconstruct that shape accurately without actually tracing it.

The drawing-machine as such is thus eventually discarded, except for demonstration purposes, but it survives in perspective as a theoretical apparatus (Fig. 11).

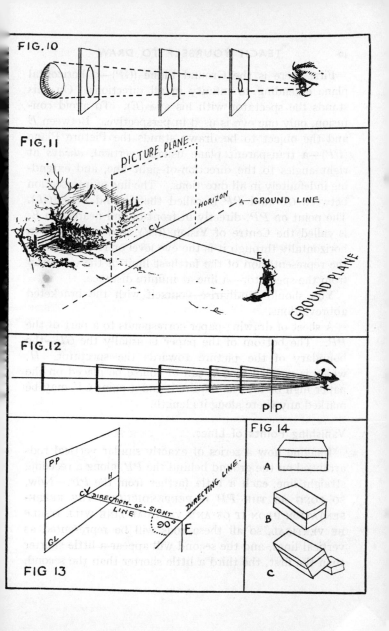

FIG. 10

FIG. 11

PICTURE PLANE

HORIZON

GROUND LINE

CV

E

GROUND PLANE

FIG. 12

PP

FIG. 13

PP

H

CV

DIRECTION-OF-SIGHT LINE

DIRECTING LINE

GL

90°

E

FIG. 14

A

B

C

First there is the Ground Plane (*GP*)—a horizontal plane extending to infinity in all directions. On this stands the spectator with his eye (*E*). To avoid confusion, only one eye is used in perspective. Between *E* and the object to be drawn stands the Picture Plane (*PP*)—a transparent plane usually vertical, *always* at right angles to the direction-of-sight line, and extending indefinitely in all directions. The line of intersection between *GP* and *PP* is called the Ground Line (*GL*). The point on *PP*, directly in front of and nearest to *E*, is called the Centre of Vision (*CV*), and a line drawn horizontally through it is the eye level or Horizon (*H*)— the representation of the farthest limit of the *GP* away from the spectator—a line at infinite distance.

You should familiarise yourself with the bracketed abbreviations.

A sheet of drawing-paper corresponds to a part of the *PP*. The bottom of the paper is usually the *GL*—the boundary of the picture towards the spectator. *H*, which is parallel to *GL*, can of course be placed on the paper high or low, as required, and a point *CV* may be marked anywhere along its length.

Vanishing Points of Lines.

Imagine now a series of exactly similar vertical rods arranged on the ground behind the *PP*, along a receding straight line, each a little farther from the *PP*. Now, SO LONG AS THE *PP* IS PERPENDICULAR, THE REPRESENTATION UPON IT OF ANY VERTICAL LINE WILL ITSELF BE VERTICAL, so all these rods will be represented as vertical lines, and the second will appear a little shorter than the first, the third a little shorter than the second,

and so on until, at infinite distance—*i.e.*, on the horizon—
a rod will appear to have no height at all; the visual rays
from its extremities to the eye will coincide (Fig. 12) and
trace it on the *PP* as a single point.

But such a series of equal heights represents the constant distance between two parallel lines—a distance
which, in perspective, must then appear to diminish
regularly until, at infinity, it vanishes altogether, so that
the parallel lines appear to meet.

From this comes the first and most important rule of
perspective, which at once enables us to give an effect of
recession :

RECEDING PARALLEL LINES APPEAR TO CONVERGE AND
TO MEET IN A POINT AT INFINITE DISTANCE.

This point is called the vanishing point of the lines
(*VP*).

RECEDING HORIZONTAL LINES HAVE THEIR *VP*s ON THE
HORIZON.

It must be clearly understood that the horizon is always
eye level. If the viewpoint is high, the horizon is high;
if it is low, the horizon is low, and the apparent distance
between *GL* and *H* is greater or smaller accordingly.
Compare, for example, the views of the sea obtained from
low beach and high cliff.

Any change of eye level alters the appearance of an
object between the extremes of a worm's eye and a bird's
eye view.

It follows that if you are making a picture whose chief
interest lies below the eye level, this should be placed
high on the paper. If, however, the chief interest is in
tall buildings, trees or clouds—in things above the eye
level—it should be placed low. It should never be

placed exactly half way between the top and bottom of the paper.

A low eye level makes things look more important or, as an artist would probably say, more monumental.

You can see the truth of the rule of vanishing points in any fairly long, straight road. All the parallel horizontal lines appear to converge towards a point on the horizon. Those above the eye level—telegraph wires, eaves and imaginary lines joining tops of lamp-posts— go down towards the *VP*, while those below eye level— kerbstones, tram-lines, window-sills, etc.—appear to go up to it.

When you are drawing such things, however, you must beware of taking receding lines too near their *VP*s. The first half-inch along a foreshortened line may represent three feet, the next perhaps twice as much, and not much farther along, a half-inch may cover several miles. The *VP*, you must remember, is at infinite distance—a very long way !

Finding a Vanishing Point.

If a line is drawn from your eye to the vanishing point of any existing line, the two must, we know, be parallel. Conversely, if from your eye a line is drawn parallel to a line whose *VP* you require, this will be found for you automatically.

The practical application of this is obvious. If you are working in a street and you wish to draw a series of receding kerb stones, or tram lines, you can close one eye, look along a line parallel to them, and actually " see " their vanishing point. This will probably coincide with the corner of a window frame or some other clearly defined point, and you will be able to plot it at the corresponding point on your drawing.

Vanishing Point of Lines receding directly into the Picture.

Imagine a line drawn through E in the perspective apparatus, horizontal and parallel to the PP (Fig. 13). This is called the Directing Line (DL).

A line drawn from E at 90° with the PP (*i.e.*, at 90° with the DL, which is parallel to PP) will give us the VP of all other lines which are at 90° with the PP. But the direction-of-sight line from E cutting PP in CV is also at 90° with the PP. CV must therefore be the VP required—the VP of all lines which are at 90° with the PP.

Parallel Perspective.

If two sides of a square on the GP are inclined to the PP at 90°—*i.e.*, vanishing to CV, the other two sides must be parallel to the PP—to the lines on one's paper representing H and GL.

The square is said to lie in parallel perspective.

Any rectangular object with one face parallel to PP is in parallel perspective (Fig. 14A).

Only the one VP is involved.

Angular Perspective.

If the square is turned so that no side is parallel to the PP, it will have two sets of receding lines and there must be two VPs.

It is said then to lie in angular perspective.

Any rectangular solid which has one face parallel to

the *GP* but none parallel to the *PP* is in angular perspective (Fig. 14B).

The *VP*s of the two sets of lines in such an object would be plotted on the *PP* by drawing vanishing parallel lines to right and left from *E*, each inclined to *DL* as required. Obviously there would be an angle of 90° between these lines at *E* and the *VP*s will be a considerable distance apart. One or both must fall off one's paper. If both are brought on to it, the perspective representation of the object will be distorted and look ridiculous.

Oblique Perspective.

A rectangular object is in oblique perspective when none of its sides is parallel to *GP* or *PP* (Fig. 14C).

Distance Points.

The two *VP*s of horizontal lines inclined to *PP* at 45° are very important points indeed, for they can be used to measure distances into the picture : hence their more usual name DISTANCE POINTS (*DP*). They are, of course, vanishing points for the diagonals of squares lying horizontally in parallel perspective.

They can be plotted by drawing vanishing parallel lines from *E* inclined to *DL* at 45° left and right. They are found, however, to be equidistant from *CV* and this distance *CV*. *DP* is equal to the distance between *E* and *CV*. A simpler method of plotting them is thus indicated.

Lines which lie on the Picture Plane, in any direction, can be actually measured with a ruler. On a sheet of paper one must make any such measurements to a convenient scale—one inch to one foot, for example.

Since five or six feet is the normal height of one's eye

above the ground, the H is placed five or six inches above the GL.

The distance of the spectator from the PP is then decided and is struck off—to scale, of course—on either side of the CV, to give a DP on the left, which we will call DP 1, and another on the right, which we will call DP 2. Unless you are using a very large sheet of paper or a very small scale, one or both of these DPs should lie off it.

They may, however, be plotted on your drawing-board or, if that is not large enough, your paper could be pinned on a wall or floor and the DPs plotted well out on that. In either case they will fall on the H line produced.

Since they are used, as you will see presently, so very frequently, these DPs may conveniently be marked with a pin or nail. On each pin is tied a length of cotton which can be pulled taut through any point on the paper to show at a glance the direction taken by a line inclined at 45° to left or right from that point.

Suppose, now, that on any line AB which lies on the GP, parallel to PP, we have to complete a square. Lines can be drawn back from A and B to CV, giving us the direction of the second and third sides of the square (Fig. 15). The fourth side we cannot draw until we have measured, along one of the receding lines, a distance equal to AB.

From A draw a line back to DP 1, cutting the line $B.CV$ in D. Then AD is the diagonal of the required square. Through D draw a line parallel to AB, cutting $A.CV$ in F. The figure $ABDF$ is the accurate perspective representation of the square.

The same result would have been achieved by drawing a diagonal from B to DP 2.

Suppose again that we require a point on *GP* four feet to the right of the spectator and two feet inside the picture. Drop a perpendicular from *CV* on to the *GL* meeting it in *X* (Fig. 16). Any point on the *GP* to the right of this line must lie to the right of the spectator, and any point on the left of it must lie to his left. Make a point *A* on *GL* four feet to the right of *X*—to scale, of course. Draw a line from *A* to *CV*. Any point on this line must lie four feet to the right of the spectator.

Make a point *B* on *GL* two feet left of *A*. Draw a line from *B* to *DP* 2 (*VP* 45°), cutting the line *A.CV* in *C*.

The triangle *ABC* is now half a square and *AC* is equal in length to *AB*.

The point *C* must therefore lie four feet to the right of the spectator and two feet inside the picture.

Any other point may be accurately placed on the *GP* in exactly the same way, providing that we know its distance to the right or left of the spectator and its distance inside the picture.

This leads us to a device which, although it has no application to freehand drawing, is most useful when one is building up a picture.

The Perspective Scale.

A point *A* is placed on *GL* one foot to the right or left of *X* (Fig. 17). It is joined to the *CV*. The lines *A.CV* and *X.CV* are now tracings of lines on the *GP*, each inclined at 90° with the *GL* and one foot apart. By using one of the *DP*s we can draw a line from *X* which will mark off a perspective foot *AY* along *ACV*. Through *Y* a line is drawn parallel to the *GL* cutting *XCV* in *Z*, and a square is formed.

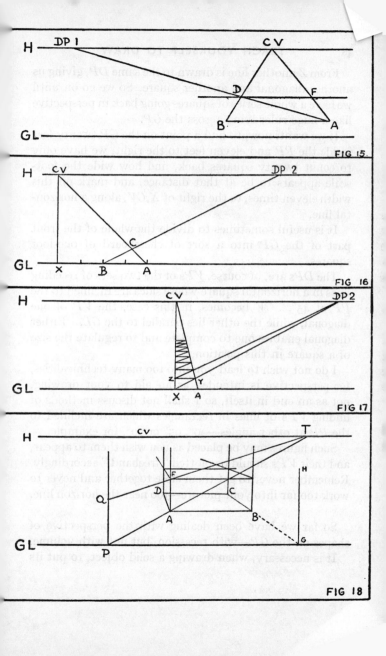

H DP 1   C V

                              D   F

                          B   A
GL
FIG 15

H   CV   DP 2

                          C
GL X   B   A
FIG 16

H   CV   DP 2

                              Z Y
GL   X
FIG 17

H   CV   T

                    F
              Q   D   C   H
              A   C
                                        B
GL P   G
FIG 18

From Z another line is drawn to the same DP, giving us another diagonal and another square. So we go on until we have a whole series of squares going back in perspective like a huge ruler lying across the GP.

If we want, now, to find a point on the GP twenty feet inside the PP and eleven feet to the right, we have only to count twenty squares back, find how wide the foot-scale appears to be at that distance, and mark off this width eleven times, to the right of $X.CV$, along a horizontal line.

It is useful sometimes to divide the whole of the front part of the GP into a sort of chessboard of one-foot squares.

The DPs are, of course, VPs of the two sets of receding lines in a horizontal square whose sides are inclined to the PP at 45°. CV becomes, in this case, the VP of one diagonal, while the other lies parallel to the GL. Either diagonal enables one to complete and to regulate the size of a square in this position.

I do not wish to lead you into too many technicalities, for perspective is intended as an aid to your drawing, not as an end in itself, so I shall not discuss methods of finding VPs of lines in rectangles which are inclined to the PP at other angles—30°, 65° or 70°, for example.

Such figures may be placed as you wish them to appear, and their VPs should be plotted " freehand " accordingly. Remember never to get them close together and never to work too far into your picture—too near the horizon line.

So far we have been dealing with the perspective of shapes on the GP—with recession, but not with volume.

It is necessary, when drawing a solid object, to put its

plan into perspective first. It does not matter what it is
or how far above the ground it may be, its plan is drawn
first. The object is then built up from this plan by raising points and lines to the required height. This is a
good method to adopt even when you are drawing freehand.

If you take any drawing which has been completed
without due consideration of plan and you reverse this
process by dropping lines and points until the base of
each object is revealed on the ground, you may very well
find that the bases of two solid objects overlap in a quite
impossible way. This is not an uncommon mistake, and
it is only to be avoided by a very systematic and
analytical approach.

The Line of Heights.

If we have in perspective the plan, $ABCD$, of a rectangular box (Fig. 18), vertical lines must be drawn from
A, B, C and D. Then from any point T on the horizon
a line is drawn through the most convenient of these
points (in this case it would be A) until it cuts the GL in
P. At P draw a vertical line. This line is, of course, in
the PP, so it can be measured directly with a rule. Set
off on it, to scale, PQ—the required height of the box.
Join Q to the point T cutting the vertical line on A in F.
PT and QT now represent two receding parallel lines, so
AF must be equal to PQ.

Lines are drawn from F to the VPs established for the
base until they cut the verticals on B and D. From these
points of intersection the remaining two sides of the " lid "
are drawn to their VPs. These two sides will intersect in
a point vertically above C, and the box will be complete.

Point T is usually called the Vertical Measuring Point (VMP), and PQ the Line of Heights.

If we had decided to let one of the VPs be the VMP, GH could have been the line of heights. By this means, of course, we should measure two vertical lines at once.

Accidental Vanishing Points (AVPs).

One frequently encounters in a picture, surfaces which are inclined to the horizontal—roofs, ramps, ladders, etc. The parallel straight lines which bound or lie on these surfaces appear to converge towards a point at infinite distance, just like horizontal parallel lines, but their VPs, or Accidental Vanishing Points, as they are called, lie above or below the horizon—not on it.

If a road is going uphill, its sides will appear to go towards an AVP above the horizon. The sides of a road going downhill will converge on a point below the horizon. These AVPs lie near to or far from H as the inclination is slight or steep. They lie vertically above or below the VP, which gives the general direction of a line —*e.g.*, if a road is to rise straight into the picture, its AVP will be vertically above CV; if it descends to the right at 45°, its AVP will be vertically beneath DP 2. Try to draw a road which sets off horizontally into the picture, towards CV, then turns slightly right or left towards a VP on the H not far from CV, then rises slightly towards an AVP, and continues gradually rising and turning at the same time. Each AVP will be a little higher than the last and a little farther to the right or left. Then take the road over a hill until it disappears.

Remember that some parallel lines, even in an inclined

plane, will continue to go towards a *VP* on *H*—the rungs of a ladder, for example, and the horizontal lines of slates on a roof.

Construction Lines.

Once you are able to set up rectangular solids anywhere in the space behind your Picture Plane, you will be able to convert them quite easily into any other form that you may require.

A roof can be added, for example, to make a simple house (Fig. 19A). Draw the diagonals of the two end rectangles. Raise vertical lines through their points of intersection. These lines will bisect the ends, but, because of foreshortening, the " half " nearest to you will appear larger than the half which is farther away. Produce these verticals upwards, and set off on the foremost the required height of the roof-top. Draw a line from there towards the *VP* of the eaves until it cuts the farther vertical line. Join the appropriate points to complete the roof. A pyramid can be built by drawing the diagonals of a square lying on the *GP*, raising a vertical line at their point of intersection and joining the top of it to the four corners of the square.

Fig. 19B shows how a circle can be drawn in perspective by using a square as " scaffolding ". This enables one to draw cylinders, arches, etc.

A cone can be drawn by using the construction for a pyramid and inscribing a circle in the square base (Fig. 19C).

There are many such simple constructions—all very useful indeed, even in freehand drawing. All construction lines of objects should be lightly drawn, even though, in the objects themselves, they are hidden.

The Application of Perspective to Picture-making.

1. The usefulness of much of this science will have become apparent in your reading. Your freehand drawing will be greatly improved by an understanding of the principles of foreshortening. Perspective scales, lines of height and the various mechanical devices cannot be employed usefully in this work, but, if you do several carefully ruled and measured exercises with them, you will be less likely afterwards to distort angles and to misjudge distances along foreshortened lines.

In this connection it is useful to remember that an object twice as far from the eye as another exactly similar object appears to be half as tall; if it is three times as far away, it appears one-third as tall; if it is four times as far away, one-quarter as tall and so on.

2. When you turn from freehand studies to the construction of a " studio " picture, you may rule and measure and use any available device.

Many spontaneous-looking paintings cover a mass of construction lines which would put an engineer to shame.

First of all, you should place your horizon—high or low, as required. Then place your *CV* on the horizon ; it need not be in the centre.

Then decide your scale—how high you would wish a five- or six-foot man to be, standing just inside the picture, right against the *PP*. From that, calculate how many inches are to equal one foot on your *PP*.

You can then decide how far away from the Picture Plane you are supposed to be standing, reduce this distance to scale, and mark it off on each side of *CV* to give *DP* 1, and *DP* 2.

These will enable you to make a perspective scale or, if you prefer it, to divide the whole *GP* into foot squares.

You can then proceed to raise or lower any part of the ground, draw roads, build up banks, hollow out ditches and build up from plan your buildings, using lines of height, *CV*, *DP*s, *VP*s, *AVP*s and any constructional devices which suggest themselves.   Trees and clouds are subject to the laws of perspective, remember—so are people !

Your man in the foreground is the key to the height of any other human beings in the picture.   By a line of heights you can take his five or six feet back to any point on *GP* and find how tall a similar man would appear to be at that point.

Here I propose to stop.   In this chapter I have done little more than touch the fringe of this subject, for its ramifications are very wide indeed.   Those of you who are mathematically inclined may care to delve further into it, but there is little more to concern the artist.

To many painters perspective has been something of an inspiration, supplying them with an all-important initial impulse.   We see this in several of the Florentines, and we find it again in the work of many advanced, intellectual painters today.

For the average person, however, perspective must be, as I have already said, a means, not an end.   He should use it but not become so dependent upon it that the actual design and content of his work are determined by it. It is an excellent guide and servant, but it can become a very bad master.

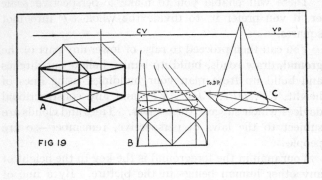

CHAPTER IV

LIGHT AND SHADE

I ADVISED you in Chapter II to " have in mind always the form of the object, to see that your shading is really expressing that form ", and I said, " It is their form which we must reconstruct, showing that they are rounded and smooth, or sharp of edge and composed of flat surfaces—that one thing is near to us, the next farther away."

How can shading help one to show all this?

How can it be made to express form?

Linear perspective will, of course, define forms and distances for us, but not with sufficient completeness and not always without ambiguity. In Fig. 20A for example, the recession is, for various reasons, so slight that one cannot tell which of the two lines *AB*, *CD*, is the nearer. In consequence, the drawing may be interpreted in several different ways—as a flat pattern of lines, as a folded screen seen from below, or as a similar screen seen from above.

In Fig. 20B shading makes it quite clear that the object is intended to be three-dimensional, but it is not clear whether the light is shining from left or right, so the drawing is still ambiguous.

Look now at Fig. 20C. It is quite clear in this drawing that certain planes face in one direction—towards the light—and that others, having no direct light on them, face the other way. This partial darkness on surfaces which the light cannot reach directly is called shade. Certain parts of the object are dark, however, not because they are turned away from light, not because they are in shade, but because the light which would normally be reaching them has been intercepted. These are the cast shadows. They have shown us from which side of this screen the light is shining, and the drawing has, now, only one possible interpretation.

Light, then, makes things visible to us in respect of their shape and colour, but it is shade and cast shadow which explain their form.

By using shade and cast shadow in a drawing we are able to give other people a true idea of the things we have seen.

When an artist is drawing with his model actually before him, he may, by careful observation (*see* page 32 —" The Drawing "), get its shade and shadows sufficiently true in shape and in relative depth to give a very complete impression of its form. He cannot always find models for the things he needs, however, and even when he is lucky in that respect, the lighting may be such that it obscures rather than explains the form, necessitating careful selection and rejection, and perhaps even an altogether new imaginary scheme of shading. He must, in short, have knowledge on which to base his selection, and be able to work out such a scheme, choosing the position for a source of light, " modelling " his drawing and projecting the cast shadows accordingly.

Notice that word " modelling " which I have just used. It is borrowed from another quite distinct branch of this

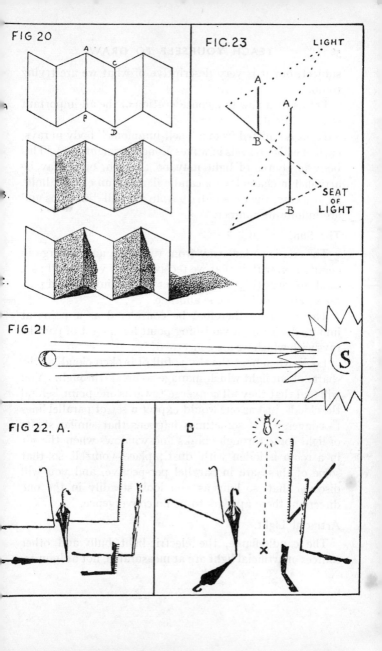

FIG 20

A C

P D

FIG.23

LIGHT

A

A

B

B

SEAT
OF
LIGHT

FIG 21

S

FIG 22, A.

B

subject, but it is very descriptive of what we are trying to do.

Let us turn now to a consideration of the all-important source of light.

Light is emitted from a " self-luminous " body in rays, each of which travels in waves along a straight line. This body or source of light may be the sun, or it may be artificial in character—a candle flame or an electric bulb. In any case, the rays radiate from it in all directions and are infinite in number.

The Sun.

The sun is so far away from the earth and so large in comparison with it that we receive only a very small part of all its rays (Fig. 21), and these, to all intents and purposes, are parallel to one another.

The sun may therefore be considered as a point at infinite distance—a vanishing point for the set of parallel rays with which we are concerned.

Look, when next the sky is full of broken cloud, at the shafts of sunlight which manage to break through. You will find that they all converge towards one point behind the clouds, just as one would expect a set of parallel lines to converge. It sometimes happens that similar shafts of light come through chinks and windows when the air in a room is laden with dust ; place yourself so that some of these are in parallel perspective, and you will discover that, so long as you look steadily in the one direction, there appears to be no convergence.

Artificial Light.

The candle-flame, the electric-light bulb and other sources of artificial light are at measurable, not at infinite, distance, and their rays, unlike those of the sun, actually appear to radiate in all directions.

If you plant a lot of sticks vertically in the ground when the sun is shining, you will find that their shadows point all in one direction; they will be parallel to one another (Fig. 22A). If, later, you put an electric light among the same sticks, their shadows will radiate—from a point on the ground directly beneath the light (Fig. 22B). This point, X, is called the seat of the luminary.

When a picture has been built up on perspective scales, VPs, DPs, etc., as explained in the preceding chapter, one may plot a point to represent the source of light—the sun or an artificial luminary—and, by drawing from it lines representing rays of light, outline the shapes of the shadows which would be cast. I will give a brief explanation of how this is done. It is usually taught as a part of perspective, although it is sometimes called Sciography—the drawing of shadows.

The Shadow of a Vertical Line Cast by an Artificial Light.

To begin with, I will suppose that we have, standing on the ground, a vertical stick, AB, whose shadow is to be cast on the ground.

You will readily understand how the position of an artificial light is determined. Having already drawn an eye-level, a ground-line, a CV and a DP, you can plot the seat of the light (*i.e.*, the point vertically beneath it on the GP). The point representing the light itself can then be raised to the required height by using a line of heights.

Now, wherever the vertical stick is situated, its shadow

will be pointing away from the seat of the luminary. Draw, from that point, then, a line passing through the bottom of the stick, B (Fig. 23). This will give the direction of the shadow. Its length will be determined by drawing a " ray " from the light through the top of the stick, A, until it cuts the shadow line.

If we had needed to cast the shadow of point A only, we should still have had to drop a line to find point B, and after that the construction would have been exactly the same.

On exactly the same principle we can find the direction and length of shadows cast by the sun ; but first we must consider the three positions in which the sun may be found.

I. The Sun in Front of the Spectator.

When the sun is in this position it will be seen on the Picture Plane, but not necessarily in that part of the plane which is occupied by one's picture.

It will be above the horizon—anywhere that you choose to place it.

It is at infinite distance so the point vertically beneath it on the ground—*i.e.*, the seat of the luminary or, as it is called in this case, the seat of the sun—will lie on the horizon.

2. The Sun in the Plane of the Picture.

When in this position, the source of light cannot be plotted at all. Its rays descend from left or right, parallel to the Picture Plane—*i.e.*, in parallel perspective—and they can be drawn parallel to one another at any desired inclination—*e.g.*, if the sun is supposed to be on the right, in the plane of the picture and at an altitude of 60°, the rays from it will be drawn parallel to one another and inclined to the horizontal at 60°.

3. The Sun Behind the Spectator.

When the sun is in this position it is not, of course, visible in the picture. Its parallel rays, however, descending from behind the spectator, passing him, and receding from him into the picture, appear to converge and to meet in a point (the Vanishing Point of the Sun's Rays—*VPSR*) which can be plotted. It is always below the horizon. If the sun is shining behind the spectator, on his right, the *VP* of its rays will be in front of him, below the horizon, on his left.

If the sun is behind him on the left, its *VP* will be in front of him, below the horizon, on his right.

In neither case can one find the seat of the luminary. Instead one raises a perpendicular to the horizon and finds the seat of the Vanishing Point of its rays.

The Shadow of a Vertical Line Cast by the Sun.

We can return now to the vertical stick, *AB*.

1. Let us cast its shadow on the ground from a sun which is in front of us and a little to our right—*i.e.*, right of *CV*—and well up in the sky (Fig. 24). If we take the sun too low the shadow will be endless. We draw now, just as we did when an artificial light was involved, a line from the seat of the luminary through *B*, on the ground. This will give us the direction of the shadow. It will, of course, be coming towards us. A ray drawn from *S* through *A* will determine the length of the shadow.

If we had a second vertical stick a good way from AB and we cast its shadow, that too would point towards the seat of the sun—*i.e.*, the two would be parallel. That, you will remember, is where shadows from the sun and shadows from artificial luminaries differ.

The seat of the sun is the vanishing point for the shadows of vertical lines on a horizontal surface.

The shadow of point A alone would have to be cast in exactly the same way.

2. Let us now cast its shadow from a sun on our left in the plane of the picture. The seat of the sun is on the ground, in the Picture Plane—at infinite distance—on our left. In other words, it lies on the GL, and if we are to draw a line going towards or away from it, we must draw it parallel to GL. Through B, then, draw a line going to the right parallel with GL (Fig. 25). This gives us the direction of the shadow. A ray drawn through A, descending from the left at an angle equal to the altitude of the sun, will cut off the shadow to the correct length.

3. When the sun is behind the spectator, the shadow of a vertical line on the ground will be going away from him. The seat on the horizon of $VPSR$ will be its vanishing point.

Let the sun be situated behind the spectator on his left and at a fair height. Its $VPSR$ will lie on the right of CV and a fair way below the horizon (Fig. 26). From B, towards the seat of $VPSR$, draw a line. This gives the direction of the required shadow. Through A, towards the $VPSR$ itself, draw a ray (from the sun behind the spectator, of course) until it cuts the shadow and so determines its length.

Shadows of Solid Objects.

Supposing now that we wish to cast the shadow of a solid object bounded wholly by planes, from an artificial luminary or from the sun in any of its possible positions. It might, of course, be a house, a shed, a table, a chair or just a geometrical object like a cube or prism.

We must first select a number of points whose shadows are certain to fall on the outline of the whole shadow—important constructional points—corners of a cube, for example. Perpendiculars, if they do not already exist, are dropped from these points to the ground or to the horizontal plane upon which the object is standing, and then, as I have already explained, the shadows of the points are cast. These, joined up in correct order, give the complete outline of the shadow of the object (Fig. 27).

One must be able to visualise the required effect fairly clearly in order to see which points on the object should be selected. It is useful in this connection to imagine what the object would look like from the position of the light. The outline of it as seen from there would be the same, of course, as the outline of the shadow, and once that is known it will be clear which points one must select for casting.

Shadows of Curves.

If the shadow of a curve is to be cast, one may first cast the shadow of the square or rectangle in which it was constructed. The curve can then be inscribed in the shadow lines. Alternatively, it may be cast point by point, the shadows of these points being joined up in order. One useful fact which you would be almost certain to discover for yourself is this : If a line is parallel to

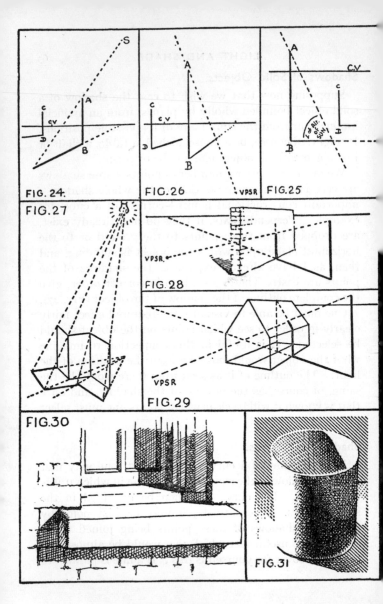

FIG. 24.

FIG. 26

FIG. 25

FIG. 27

FIG. 28

FIG. 29

FIG. 30

FIG. 31

a plane and its shadow is cast on that plane, the shadow and the line will be parallel. The shadow will go towards the *VP* of the line.

Experiment with a ruler held horizontally over a horizontal surface in strong light, and see if this is not so.

If the shadow of a square held horizontally is cast on the ground (*i.e.*, on the *GP*) by the sun, the shadow will be exactly the same in all respects as the square itself.

It follows that the shadow of a horizontal circle—*e.g.*, the top of a pillar-box or of a round table—cast by the sun on another horizontal surface, will also be a true circle.

This is not necessarily true if the shadow is cast by an artificial luminary.

The Shadow of One Object upon Another.

Suppose now that the shadow of our line *AB*, cast by the sun or by an artificial luminary in any position, runs along the ground until it encounters a vertical wall. What will happen?

The vertical line is, of course, parallel to the vertical wall, so the shadow will go vertically up this until it is cut by the ray passing through *A* (Fig. 28).

If it goes far enough up the wall to encounter a sloping roof, the shadow will fall, in part, on the roof, and in order to determine its direction we shall have to cut an imaginary slice through the building (Fig. 29), producing the first part of the shadow along the ground until it reaches the bottom of an imaginary wall through the middle of the house. Up this wall it will go, vertically, emerging at the top at the point towards which the shadow must be taken.

C—DRAW

Continue the shadow from where it was left to this point, and determine its length by drawing a ray in the usual way.

This is a simple example of what is known as the strip method. The principle is always the same, but every time it is applied it presents a new problem.

By casting shadows of the necessary points in this way, we can obtain the shadow of one object upon another, and perhaps give to each a greater sense of solidity.

See if you can work out the method used for casting the shadow of a downstair window-sill on its wall (Fig. 30), and for drawing the shadow inside a hollow cylinder (Fig. 31). This particular cylinder is made of a translucent substance, so shadows cast inside are visible also on the outside.

So much for cast shadows. Sciography, like perspective, can be taken much farther than I am able to take it here, but you have already enough to be of very great use—enough to guide your analysis of the shadows in your freehand-drawing groups, and enough to enable you to invent likely shadows when you are working from memory or imagination.

Shade.

We must now consider the shade which occurs on the object itself.

Those parts of the surface of an object which are turned towards the source of light are " in light ", and the paper may be left white to show them. As they turn away from it they receive less light, and, in your drawing, more pencilling, until at last they are " in shade ".

The intermediate parts of the surface which turn

neither directly towards the light nor directly away from it are in " half-tone "—light half-tone or dark half-tone, according to whether they incline more to the light or to the shade side of the object.

The pencil is able to express perfectly these subtle tones or gradations between white and black.

On rounded surfaces the light merges gradually into shade through half-tones; on angular forms the transition between light and half-tone, half-tone and shade, or between light and dark is abrupt. Compare Figs. 32A and B, C and D, E and F, G and H, in each of which the sun is shining down from the left-hand side, in the plane of the picture.

I use geometrical solids as examples because they show an effect so clearly and because natural forms are so easily reduced into terms of them. If, for example, you are drawing an arm, a neck or a tree-trunk, and you know, or can work out, how a cylinder would look in the same lighting, your task will be greatly simplified. The shading on a head will be generally similar to that on a sphere, and other, smaller geometrical shapes will be encountered in the features—e.g., a half cone. The shading on a fir-cone, though much broken up by smaller forms, will be generally that of a cone; so might the shading on the fir tree itself.

The direction of light must always be arranged, of course, so that it shall best explain the form of an object. Move the light round a little in Fig. 32C, for example, removing the half-tone, and the drawing would not be nearly so clear.

In each of these diagrams the shading leaves no doubt at all of the form of the object. The pencilling in Fig.

33A, however, serves no useful purpose at all, yet it is typical of the uniform greyness which some students call shading. Another common mistake is seen in Fig. 33B—a cube on which the light is supposed to be shining from the right : one part of one side is put in light because it is near to the light, and the rest is put in shade. This never happens. A plane in shade is all in shade.

Some people find difficulty in deciding which parts of the surface will be in light. They should try to imagine, again, what the object looks like from the position of the luminary. Everything—all surfaces which could be seen from there—would be in light, while all those which were out of sight would be in shade, or half-tone.

Sometimes the plan of an object can be drawn roughly, and also the plan of the rays illuminating it. Figs. 34 and 35 are plans of the cylinder and prism in Figs. 32D and 32C. It is clear which parts of these objects are reached by the rays of light and which will be in shade. The rays, A and B, passing *along* surfaces produce the half-tones.

These plans suggest also that the surfaces turned most directly towards the light will be lightest of all. There is, for example, one spot in the light side of a sphere—at the centre of it and nearest the luminary—which is lighter than any other.

When a sphere or a vertical cylinder is illuminated by the sun, whose rays, you will remember are parallel, exactly one-half of its surface is in shade. You will see this in Fig. 34. Look also, when the sun is shining very brightly, at one of the white stone balls which sometimes adorn the gate-pillars of houses; you will see very clearly the division into half-light, half-shade.

If the same objects were illuminated by an artificial luminary whose rays diverge from their source, the light area would be rather smaller than the shade. The difference is so slight, however, as to be of little concern in practice. The amount of light and shade that you actually see from one position depends, of course, on the position of the luminary. You will notice that the shaded half of an object is never dead black—never entirely devoid of light. Look again at the objects with curved surfaces in Figs. 32B, D and F. The light on these goes into half-tone and then into shade, and then, as the surface turns out of sight, it becomes a little lighter again. You will find a similar lightening in the shade side of the angular solids. This heightening—*i.e.*, lightening—of tone is caused by reflected light.

Reflected Light.

Rays of light illuminate those surfaces of an object which are turned towards their source and are reflected from them in all directions. Some of these reflected rays as we have seen, converge on the eye, and make us aware of the existence of the object. Others find their way into shadows and the shaded surfaces of other objects.

A certain amount of light is reflected, thus, from the ground, and although it is not nearly so strong as direct light, it does give an object a greater sense of solidity. A sphere or a cylinder, for example, whose shading is not relieved by a little reflected light from the ground or from some adjacent surface appears to have a sharp edge and not to turn away at all.

Reflected light enables one to model forms which would

otherwise be invisible in shadow. It gives them a low-toned light side, a slightly darker shade side and even a faint shadow—all in reverse, of course, to the main scheme of lighting (*see* the lettering in Fig. 32H).

Cast shadows, especially outdoors, receive little reflected light, and are therefore nearly always darker than the shade side of the object which is casting them. They nearly always appear darker, however, by contrast, where they are directly adjacent to a light surface—*i.e.*, along their edges.

The shade or half-tone sides of an angular solid similarly appear darker along the edges which are in contact with the light side. If these edges are shaded rather darker in a drawing, the change of direction between the two planes will be emphasised.

The corresponding edges of the light side will appear a little lighter from the contrast, so, to increase still further the illusion of solidity, the light side itself may be shaded slightly away from these edges (Fig. 36).

This must be done very subtly, however. The light side and the shade side must be clearly differentiated : no small lights should be allowed to break up the shade side, nor any small pieces of shading the light side.

The half-tones should be considered part of the light side ; their darkness should not encroach too far upon it.

It helps one considerably in one's task of expressing form to imagine sections cut at intervals through the object which is being drawn. Fig. 37, of the trunk of a tree, will best explain this.

Much meaningless shading is avoided by this method. It is equally well applied to legs and arms and to the delicate stems of flowers, as we shall see later.

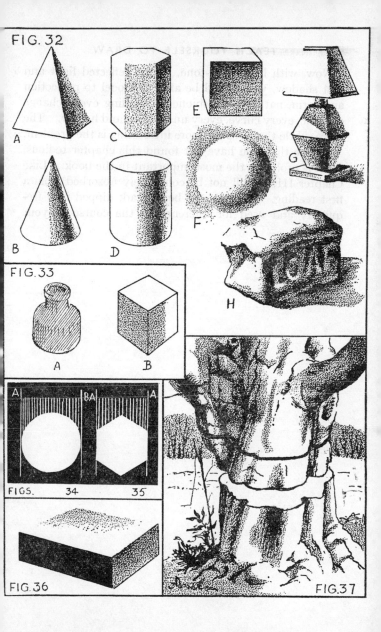

FIG. 32

FIG. 33

FIGS. 34 35

FIG. 36

FIG. 37

Now, with light, half-tone, shade, reflected light and cast shadow, you should be able to model to perfection any form, natural or fashioned, revealing every change of plane, every curve, every undulation and hollow. The more subtle the form the more interesting is the problem.

I hope that you have not found this chapter tedious, for it is probably the most important in the book. Like Chapter III, it will not be completely absorbed from a first reading. Both should be re-read, dipped into frequently and used for reference in the course of your drawing.

CHAPTER V

OBJECT DRAWING—CONCLUSION

I WANT you to turn now to Plate I and, if you have been able to make models of your own, to arrange them in exactly the same way.

All the objects are white. The cardboard " chimney ", which was sent to me round a roll of lino, and the piece of corrugated packing-paper which stands like a fence in front of the flight of steps, were once brown, but several coats of white poster paint have brought them into line.

The background consists of a piece of black cloth pinned to a clothes-horse.

The group is set up on a card-table covered with white paper. My eyes, when I sit down to draw, are just above the level of the eaves of the house—in the same position as the lens of the camera with which this photograph was taken. The models were arranged in several different ways before I finally decided that this grouping would be the most satisfactory for our purpose. The lighting had then to be carefully considered. A single electric lamp was placed in front and to the right of the group and, to avoid double shadows, all other light was excluded from the room. Shadows equally sharp and clear are obtained if a group is arranged in the sun, but they change very quickly. When the lamp was raised a little, the roof of the house received as much light as the front wall, and the whole thing looked flat; when it was moved to the left, no shade could be seen on the chimney and the open door came into light. In its present position the light casts good interesting shadows and explains very well every change of plane.

With this group as model, I am going to describe various stages in the making of a pencil-drawing, showing how some of the suggestions and rules given in previous chapters may be applied.

The camera sometimes fails to record subtle variations in tone which are apparent to the eye; they may also be lost in the reproduction of a photograph, so you should refer, while you are reading this chapter, not to Plate I alone, but to the group of models which you have made and arranged yourself.

Before you set pencil to paper, the group must be studied carefully, perhaps for a considerable time. Its perspective and its light and shade must be analysed mentally, and you must see quite clearly, before you begin drawing, what you have to do and how you are going to set about it.

A pencil held at arm's length, first vertically, then horizontally, confirms your impression that the length of the group is greater than its height. Your paper will therefore be used with the short side vertical.

The pencil, again extended horizontally at the height of your eyes, shows that eye-level is above the eaves and about a third of the way up the roof of the house.

All the objects in the group are in the same angular perspective, so there are two sets of receding parallel lines with vanishing points on the eye-level. Both these

vanishing points will fall off your paper, one on the right—
a long way away—the other on the left—much nearer.
All other straight lines in the group, with the exception
of four, are vertical. The exceptions are the inclined
lines at the ends of the roof, three of which are visible,
and the bottom of the open door. The lines in the roof
go towards accidental vanishing points, but they can
be made to converge sufficiently if the roof is built up
from a plan of the model. The direction of the bottom
of the door can be judged quite easily.

The position of the luminary should now be considered,
and you must discover why the shaded parts of the
model vary so much in tone. The front of the house,
the side of the steps, the right side of the chimney and
the extreme end of the corrugated fence are turned most
directly towards the source of light, and these are the
brightest parts of the group. If you could see the hidden
end of the house and the other side of the projecting wall,
they would probably be lighter still.

The roof, though in light, is beginning to turn away
from the source, and it is appreciably darker. The
ground, the top of each step and the landing—all horizontal planes—are in dark half-tone. The open door is
also in half-tone, but it bends slightly at the bottom and
picks up a little more light. The curved surfaces of the
chimney and of the corrugated fence turn gradually
away from the source of light and pass through half-
tones into shade.

The end wall of the house, that part of the under side
of the roof which is visible, the rise of each step, the
projecting wall and the left-hand side of both chimney
and fence are in shade, and any light which they receive

is reflected into them from other surfaces. Light is reflected from the wall of my room into the end of the house; from the front wall of the house into the rise and tread of each step; from the side of the flight of steps into the projecting wall and the shade side of the corrugated fence. Each of these corrugations is part of a cylinder and each has its light and shade side, half-tone and reflected light. As direct light on these corrugations decreases, the reflected light from the wall increases. The glow at the end of the fence will be seen to consist of thin lines of subdued light separated by delicate lines of shade. The reflected light on the left-hand side of the chimney comes from the hidden wall of the house and the roof. It is broken because the roof casts a shadow on the side wall.

Reflected light must not, of course, be allowed to break up a shade side—making it look like a half-tone.

The cast shadows remain to be considered. The shadows of the steps on the wall of the house receive little reflected light from the shaded surfaces which surround them, and their darkness is emphasised by the lightness of the wall. The shadows cast by the projecting wall on the corrugated fence and on the side of the steps are very dark for the same reason; so is the shadow at the top of the open door. The shadow of the fence on the side of the steps is not so dark, because the corrugations send some of their reflected light into it. The shadow of each step on the tread of the next is so full of light, reflected from the wall of the house, that the change of plane between rise and tread is lost. You must show this change, in a drawing, by making the shadow a little darker. The roof casts a shadow on the top of the wall,

but there is such a glow of reflected light under the eaves
that this shadow becomes a thin line of dark half-tone.
You will notice, also, that several of the corrugations in
the fence cast thin shadows on their next-door neighbours.

As soon as this preliminary analysis is complete and
you are satisfied that your course is clear, pin your paper
on to the board and proceed.

First draw a " frame ", unless, of course, your paper is
the right size and shape and you prefer to work right up
to the edges of it. Then indicate, very lightly, the size
and position of the group so that you can draw the
horizon. Still very lightly, draw the back of the table
and the plan of the objects; be sure to draw the *apparent*
length and direction of all these lines. You need not
plot vanishing points of receding lines, so long as you
can guess at their positions on the eye-line and draw the
lines towards them. You will be less likely to make
mistakes here if all converging lines are produced a little
way (Fig. 38).

Next raise all the vertical lines to the required height
and complete the construction, continually adjusting the
whole thing, including the plan, until you are satisfied
with it. See, for example, that the right side of the
chimney, behind the projecting wall, is vertically above
the end of the corrugated fence and that the right side of
the doorway is vertically above the other end of the
fence. The point of the roof must come just in front of
the chimney.

Fig. 38 gives some idea of what the drawing will look
like at this stage, but the lines should be only just visible.

The roof may be constructed by drawing the diagonals

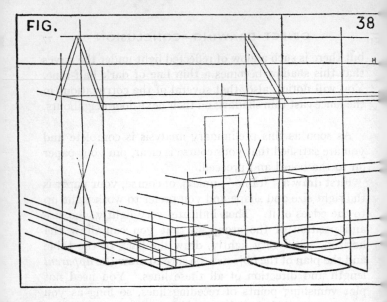

FIG. 38

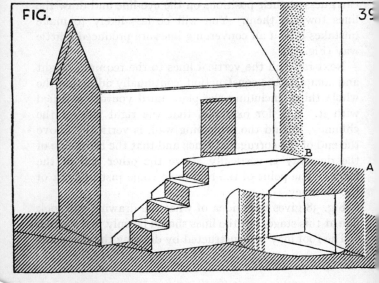

FIG. 39

of rectangles at each end of the house and by raising vertical lines through their points of intersection (Chapter 3 and Figs. 19 and 38), but you must keep comparing your drawing with the group.

Almost before this constructional drawing is complete you should indicate all the planes which are in shade, making them about equal in tone to the lightest reflected light and blending the half-tones, on curved surfaces, into the light (Fig. 39).

The outlines of the cast shadows should be drawn next (Fig. 39). Shadows of vertical lines on horizontal planes—on the ground and on the treads of the steps— come first. Then, where these encounter vertical planes, they may be drawn vertically up them. The shadow of the front edge of the projecting wall runs along the ground, up and over the corrugated fence, along the ground again, and up the side of the steps. Soon after it comes into sight the ray which passes through point A (Fig. 39) cuts it, and the shadow of the top of the wall returns to point B. The whole outline of the shadow should be drawn, very lightly, although some of it will later be hidden.

The shadow of each step crosses the tread of the next and then runs vertically up the wall of the house. You need not actually draw rays from the luminary, but you should analyse the shapes of all the shadows in the group and reconstruct them—freehand.

You will now have a sound foundation upon which to " model " your drawing. First bring all the shadows and shaded planes up to their full strength, according to the observations which you made in your preliminary analysis. Make the end of the house darker than the roof; put the horizontal planes into dark half-tone, and so on (Fig. 40). Everything that you add must really help to explain the form of the group. Bits of shading which serve no particular purpose are redundant, if not positively harmful. Things which are destructive, like the reflected light on the treads of the steps, should be modified or left out altogether.

Reflections of the dark door and the wall which appear in the shiny surface of the landing may be introduced into your drawing or completely ignored. The break in the reflected light on the chimney is useful because it helps to show that the chimney is behind the point of the roof.

The light and shade on the corrugated fence is very pleasing. It is a passage of rich texture in an otherwise severe composition. You should think about it and draw it very deliberately.

Finally you can accentuate changes of plane and increase the apparent solidity of the drawing by forcing out certain edges. Shaded planes can be made a little darker along those edges which adjoin light planes (Chapter IV). The end wall of the house appears very dark, by contrast, where it meets the brilliant front wall. The roof, too, can be darkened slightly as it descends.

The landing and the rises and treads of all the steps get gradually darker as they come towards the front.

The corresponding edges of the light planes appear a little lighter by contrast, and, in certain circumstances, the light side itself may be shaded gently away from these edges. I must repeat, however, that this has to be done very carefully. The light and shade sides must be clearly differentiated.

The ground will appear to lie down and to recede if you darken it gradually towards the front of the picture.

The sheet of black cloth which forms a background to this group looks very well in the photograph, but you would not attempt to imitate it in a drawing. A mass of black lead is shiny and unpleasant and, in any case, colour has no place in a drawing. A little conventional shading may sometimes be placed against the edge of any light plane which seems to disappear into the white background (Fig. 40). Such shading should be just dark enough to throw the edge of the plane into relief, and it should, on the other side, blend imperceptibly into the paper.

Line may play a greater part in some groups than it does in this one, but you should set about any collection of solid objects, natural or fashioned, in exactly the same way.

Drawing and shading earnestly, with mind and eyes fixed more upon your subject than upon your paper, intent upon understanding it, getting absolutely everything essential out of it, you will gradually forget that your paper is flat and that your pencil is capable of making an even, unexpressive line. You will *feel* it all in terms of space and solidity; the laws and rules of light and shade and perspective, and all your technical devices will be absorbed into an intuitive appreciation of form, and you will have in your keeping a perfect instrument for the expression, not only of ideas born in your own mind, but of the essential structural idea which exists in your subject.

Only draw and keep on drawing; draw anything and everything—in the same searching, patient way in which you begin. Never attempt to be slick. Slickness is not your goal—nor is finish, unless you can remember that greater finish is greater truth and not merely a tidying-up process.

Finally, when you turn from this indoor work to " seek fresh woods and pastures new ", don't be tempted to go out sketching. Go and make drawings from Nature; draw whatever interests you, and stress in your drawing that aspect of your subject which first attracts you; let your drawing take ten hours or ten minutes, but don't sketch.

To sketch implies aimlessness, slickness and a certain untidiness of mind. In your drawings, however slight, every line should be disciplined, studied, charged with meaning; " A line is the track of a thought ", we are told, and it is certainly the thought in a drawing which makes it worth while.

CHAPTER VI

DRAWING OUTDOORS

THE indoor work with which this book has so far been
concerned may be undertaken at any time of the year,
but it is most conveniently kept for the winter months.
It is unwise to attempt outdoor work between October
and April, except in unusual circumstances, but when
the warm light days of late spring and early summer
arrive, you will wish, very wisely, to leave your object
drawing and to spend as much time as possible in the
open air.

Drawing outdoors may well bring you for the first
time into really close touch with Nature. If you sit
quietly in one place for an hour or two on end, as one
must when drawing, you will find that the birds and
small wild creatures get quite used to your presence
and go about their business as though you were not
there. I always find this immensely gratifying.

Drawing widens your horizon in more ways than
this, however. It will cause you to look with new
interest at horses, houses, carts, people and everything
which comes within your field of vision. It is linked
so closely, too, with other human activities that you
may get more from the books you read, from the theatre
and the films; you may, through interest in the *décor*,

develop a taste for ballet and, from wishing to understand better the things you draw, you may acquire some knowledge of cattle and agriculture, of ships, architecture or the circus.

You need not, however, stray far afield in search of subject-matter. You should find something near at hand and settle down to it as quickly as you can. If you look too long for a subject, you will find yourself bewildered by the wealth of material which is there for the choosing.

Don't be too ambitious: resist any temptation to draw wide panoramic views, and avoid for the present anything which is moving.

You will be wise to draw, first of all, objects which are similar to the models you have been studying indoors—houses, bridges, barns and sheds. The difference in scale between real and model buildings may trouble you a little at first and, since your " group " is no longer conveniently isolated from its surroundings, you will have to decide how much of the subject should be included in a drawing and how it is to be placed on your paper. Some people use for this purpose a sheet of card in which is cut a small aperture the shape of their drawing-paper. They shut one eye and frame their subject in the aperture, moving the card about until they find an arrangement which is satisfactory. If you experience any difficulty here, you might for a time adopt this method.

You will most certainly have trouble with the light outdoors. It is much more variable than studio lighting, and in the space of half an hour the shade and shadows in your subject will change completely. You can overcome this difficulty by working on one subject for a short time on each of several successive days, between certain fixed hours when you may reasonably expect the sun to be in the same position.

Alternatively, you can draw carefully the " construction " of the subject—everything in it which does not change with the light—and then, last of all, put in the shades and shadows quite quickly, perhaps with a wash of water-colour (Chapter IX). With increasing understanding of the principles governing light and shade, however, you will not be disturbed by a complete change in the direction of light so long as the form remains constant.

Remember that you are not concerned with the colour of the things you draw—only with their form as revealed by light and shade.

One more general consideration before I deal with some of your subjects in greater detail : Do not burden yourself with unnecessary materials, particularly if your work lies at the end of a long walk. A small rucksack will take all you need—including a light board. A "fishing-bag" is even better, being more compact. You should add to your equipment a small folding stool. It need not be of the three-legged sketching-stool variety; a light metal picnic seat is very satisfactory and slips easily into one's bag. You may find, sometimes, that a wall or tree-stump gives a better view of your subject than can be obtained from this low stool. When you are sitting outdoors, the drawing-board rests on your knees and is supported by your spare hand.

Buildings.

In selecting a building or group of buildings for drawing you must not be guided by admiration for the grandiose and the picturesque. A loose arrangement of plate-layers' huts or pig-sties may have greater pictorial possibilities than the local church or civic centre. Such humble subjects are in any case preferable for the moment, because they are less awe-inspiring.

In tackling them you will need all your perspective and light and shade. Build them up freehand—no ruler should be used in drawing of this kind, indoors or out—but make use of the constructions detailed in Fig. 19 and in the accompanying text.

You should indicate the eye-level before you do anything else, even though it may eventually be completely obscured by hills or trees. Take into consideration the ground on which the buildings are standing; model it as carefully as you model the buildings themselves, and raise these from their plans. Remember, too, that cast shadows will follow the form of the ground.

You must discover all you can about the actual construction of your buildings. See first what they are made of and how the material affects their appearance. Wood produces forms entirely different from concrete or brick; thatch makes a roof which is essentially different from one made of corrugated iron. Do not force materials into doing something which is impossible. Only careful examination and analysis of the structure of your subject will prevent your making serious mistakes. Try to find a reason for the direction of the boarding in a wooden structure and for the particular arrangement of sheets of corrugated iron—where these occur. Be sure that you understand how bricks are laid—what " pattern " they make.

Be careful to get windows and doors the right size, and beware of making disproportionately large those things which seem to be of most importance. See, for example, how many brick courses lie between the top and bottom of a door. There will be more than you expect.

Try to give some idea of the texture of the surfaces you are drawing—brick, wood, roughcast, etc.—but do not worry the light side of any object with so much incidental pencil-work that it can be mistaken for shade or half-tone.

Less detail and texture are seen in an object as its distance from the spectator increases. The vertical lines of mortar between the bricks in a wall are clearly visible when you are close to them, but, from a distance, only the long, horizontal lines between the courses are visible, and eventually these also disappear and the wall appears to be quite plain.

You must take into account also the effect of atmosphere on the appearance of things (aerial perspective). It is usually laden with dust and moisture, which tend to obscure distant objects. THE MORE DISTANT THEY ARE, the more they are obscured and THE LIGHTER OR HIGHER IN TONE THEY WILL APPEAR TO BE.

In the clear early morning, before the dust has been turned up from the ground, one can see quite easily for many miles. In the evening visibility is not so good and, when it is raining and the air is full of moisture, houses and hills which are comparatively near may be completely blotted out.

The walls of your cardboard houses have practically no thickness, but you must not draw real buildings like that. An open door or window may sometimes be introduced to give a glimpse of the thickness of a wall and to show the space inside a building. Use any device which will thus increase the sense of form or emphasise a change of plane.

You will find more convergence in the parallel lines in a real building than you have found in the lines of a cardboard model. Don't overdo it, though; remember your vanishing points, and never let foreshortened lines or planes recede too far.

Buildings and Pictures.

There is no reason why you should not, now, be making some quite interesting pictures or compositions. Some you may complete outdoors; others you may build up at home from several different studies.

The drawing of buildings is, in these, of first importance. No landscape painting seems to me complete without some architectural interest. It may be only a broken wall or a distant house, but it serves to stabilise the whole and to emphasise by contrast the rhythmic qualities of trees and clouds and other natural forms.

Where buildings form the major part of a picture they must be interesting and varied in form. There must be an element of contrast somewhere in their arrangement. Curved and angular forms may be played off against each other, or a squat, ungainly object may be introduced among taller, more graceful, things. There should certainly be some large and some smaller forms, some quite static and others obviously capable of movement and growth. These must be balanced in quantity. It requires a number of small forms to balance one large form, and a large, plain surface to balance a small, richly textured one.

It is important that the spaces between forms should be considered, as well as the forms themselves. If one is giving an illusion of depth, solidity and distance, the picture must be designed in terms of these.

I have already said that the ground must be drawn and modelled as carefully as the things standing on it. It must also be designed as carefully.

A picture tackled as this book suggests may be likened, in some respects, to a stage; it is a framed space in which objects are to be arranged. The spectator must, however, feel himself able to get right into the picture, to walk about in it and, if he wishes, to go right through it. Don't shut the picture in on all sides like a closed box; leave the eye a way out.

If you always have a pencil and paper in your pocket, you will be able to make notes of the arrangement of any interesting groups of buildings that you come across. You will find them in quite unexpected places. Such drawings may need adjustment before you are able to use them, but they are usually better than anything one can invent.

The shapes made by the outlines of buildings, by their roof-lines and chimneys, should also be considered. They, too, must be interesting and varied, but do not " break them up " too much. Keep them clear and simple.

Other Static Objects Outdoors.

Pillar-boxes, lamp-posts, wagons, haystacks, boats and other static objects may be drawn at this stage, and introduced into your pictures. They will present some new difficulties; you will have trouble with the wheels of a cart, I expect, but find out all you can about their construction and take every opportunity of studying and drawing them.

Don't forget to reduce these and all other objects to their simplest geometrical terms; a wheel is part of a very shallow cylinder; the body of a cart is simply a box; the lamp-post may be a series of cylinders. Analyse everything, and reconstruct it in your drawing.

I prefer always to work in the country because there is less possibility of my being watched and interrupted in my work, and because the country offers such a wealth of subject-matter for drawing and painting. If, however, you wish to draw in a farmyard or a barn, you should first obtain the owner's permission. I make a point of doing this, and I have never yet been refused. Farmers and country people are more helpful than is generally supposed—if they are approached in the right manner.

Trees.

A tree is not likely to run away while you are drawing it, but it is not static in the sense that a building is static. Natural forces are always at work upon it, and you must try to understand them.

It may be bent nearly double by prevailing winds, or be forced away from its neighbours in search of sunlight to a quite unusual height; its growth and char-

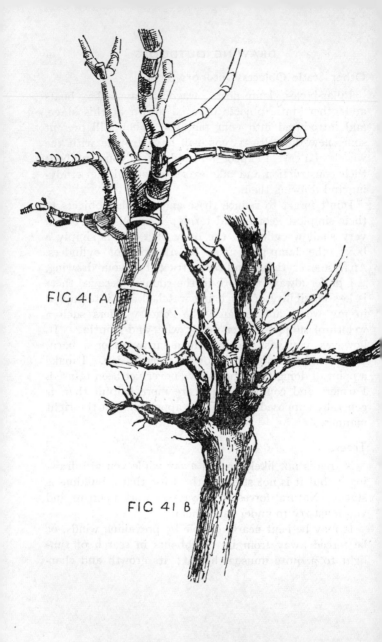

FIG 41 A.

FIG 41 B

acter may have been altered by lopping or pollarding, by lightning or disease. The tree is living and growing imperceptibly even as you watch it, and you must endeavour to get some feeling of this into your drawing.

1. From the roots, some of which may in certain trees be visible above ground, springs the trunk. This is always larger in circumference than any other part of the tree. From the trunk, gradually decreasing in girth, come the boughs, then the branches, and finally the twigs. All these parts are roughly cylindrical, and they should be drawn and shaded accordingly. Limbs which curve in growing can be reduced to a series of short cylinders at the required angles with one another—rather like cylindrical beads on a thread (Fig. 41A).

Show quite clearly, by applying your knowledge of perspective and of light and shade, which branches go away from you and which come towards you. The tree must be treated first and foremost as a solid thing. Its solidity must be emphasised.

One frequently hears of people who cannot see the wood for trees; many draughtsmen fail to see the tree for leaves! It is advisable, therefore, to make your first studies when there are no leaves to confuse you. If the weather does not permit of your sitting outdoors, you might make drawings of these bare, wintry trees from a convenient window.

See how the arrangement, direction, proportion and general character of the trunk and limbs vary in different species of tree. Compare the " skeletons " of the oak, elm, poplar and weeping-willow, for example. In some trees the branches are erect and firm, while in others they tend to droop; in some the limbs are jerky and of a " broken " character, in others they are very smooth and curvilinear.

The constructional cylinders of your tree, having served their purpose, should be adjusted to give the true section of the trunk and limbs (Fig. 41B). If your first drawing is quite faint, this will not be difficult.

The conformation of the trunk may be very important, and you should try to render it faithfully. The oak is knobbly and rugged; the beech trunk is comparatively smooth and very slightly spiral, while the surface of some tree-trunks seems to be composed entirely of small, flat planes.

The texture of the bark can be shown by drawing shadows in its hollows, each true in tone and shape and size.

Shadows cast from one branch on to another help to show the section of the second and the direction and position of both.

A book on trees, with some good photographs and botanical diagrams, will help you in this work, but painstaking study of trees themselves is essential. They will be your best teachers.

2. When a tree is in leaf, the skeleton may be almost entirely hidden, but the character and the appearance of the whole tree are nevertheless determined by it. It should be followed carefully, and where it does appear through the leaves it should be drawn.

The leaves themselves will not be considered individually unless they are drawn at very close quarters. They grow usually in well-defined masses, and these, with the general form of the whole tree, must be modelled with light, half-tone, shade, reflected light and cast shadow. Your early study of simple geometrical solids will stand you in good stead here. One tree may resemble an inverted bowl or a stunted cone; another an almost complete sphere. Some, not so simple, are combinations of several such forms. The fir is conical, the plane tree spherical, while the branches of the cedar support great, irregular layers of needles which are almost flat.

What simple forms do the following trees most closely resemble: the poplar, the oak, the horse-chestnut and the elm?

Though these basic forms should be modelled very clearly, you must not allow them to become hard and set. They are capable of rearrangement and of ceaseless, rustling movement. The wind may break them momentarily and the sky peep through. Their edges are always soft and uncertain. They are essentially leaves.

You can use your pencil in such a way that the shading will, without taking into account every tiny leaf, suggest the characteristic leafy texture of the tree.

If the forms of a tree are truthfully drawn they will inevitably produce the characteristic shape or outline, but it is advisable to keep one eye on it all the time. It is very important. A distant tree, like a distant building, loses most, if not all its detail, and is sometimes recognisable only by its shape. It also appears smaller than a similar object in the foreground and is lighter in tone.

Only long and devoted practice will give you confidence and enable you to draw a tree with any real understanding and sympathy. You alone can discover the technique which is best suited to your needs and your temperament.

Trees and Pictures.

Nearly all the advice given here on drawing and arranging the buildings in a picture will apply equally to the drawing and arranging of trees.

They need to be grouped in an interesting way and arranged not on the surface of the paper alone, but in the space behind it as well.   Their outline, like the roof-line of buildings, must be considered.   Very often buildings and trees combine to make this " line ".

Trees must take their place with the buildings in a picture, being shuffled about with them, modelled and adjusted until a satisfactory, balanced whole is arrived at.

Drawings of trees made from Nature can scarcely fail to be balanced, for every tree and every group of trees grows naturally into a perfect composition.

Plant Drawing.

When a tree or part of a tree occupies the foreground of a picture its parts must be rendered in greater detail, and you will need to make careful studies of them. These studies should be made, whenever possible, from leaves, bark, twigs, etc., which are still on the living tree, for it is impossible to arrange cut specimens in a really convincing way.

Choose, of course, some small part of the tree which is sheltered from the wind and therefore reasonably still.

Particular attention should be paid to details of growth.

Do not worry about anything which seems to be unusual or accidental unless you have some particular reason for doing so; concern yourself rather with the things which are typical of the whole species. Generalise as much as you like, and be very economical with both line and shading.

It is not a bad plan to make detailed studies of every tree that you draw. If you do this your drawings will be of much greater value as references later on.

Plants from the hedgerow, the field and the garden can be drawn in exactly the same way. They make interesting studies and are very useful when you have to deal with the immediate foreground of a picture. These, too, are best studied out of doors, in their natural setting, but some of them can be cut and arranged indoors fairly satisfactorily. A glass test-tube filled with water or wet sand will hold small specimens quite well and keep them fresh for a considerable time.

Plant drawing is not unlike object drawing. You will be able to trace in plants all the familiar basic forms—cones, cylinders, spheres, etc.—and the intention of your drawing must be exactly the same. You are still concerned with form, and not with colour. Plant-forms are usually rather delicate, however, and possessed of a very subtle rhythm, so your drawing must be very sensitive and rather restrained.

If you find this work especially congenial, you might turn it to some definite purpose. You could, for example, grow a plant from seed, in a pot, and record its changing appearance in daily drawings. You will be delighted with the unexpected beauty which such close attention will reveal. Designers sometimes fall back on this practice when they need new motifs for pattern-making.

We, in Europe, have never been so concerned with plants and flowers as the painters of the East, but here and there in our galleries and shops you will find plant drawings and paintings, and also woven and printed fabrics which bear the unmistakable stamp of great art.

The Ground.

The importance of the ground in a picture has already been twice emphasised, so I need say little more about it.

It should be treated, to begin with, as a series of planes in perspective; some are horizontal; some rise away from the spectator, others descend; some blend smoothly into one another, others remain angular, but all lead the eye gradually into the picture, towards the horizon. Before the horizon is actually reached the ground may rise, of course, into hills or mountains and completely obscure it.

Because distance makes things appear lighter, the foreground is always darker than the middle distance, and this is darker than the far distance. The effect of recession in a picture will be greatly increased if the ground is shaded gradually towards the onlooker.

Textures—furrows in a ploughed field, for example—will also emphasise the recession of the ground, but to be really effective they must be drawn carefully. Work out exactly what happens to the earth as it is cut by the coulter and turned by the breast of the plough. Make studies from " life " of cobbled roads, rutted lanes, corn-stubble and grass.

Such textures must follow the form of the ground, and they are subject to its general scheme of light and shade. Grass or corn in a field appears to get lighter the farther it is away, and when the ground is hollowed and shaded the grass which covers it is shaded also.

I am frequently asked how one should draw grass. I can only suggest that you sit in a field and put down quite honestly what you see and not what you know to be there. You cannot, obviously, draw every blade of grass in the field. Look at the far side of it; you will find that there you can see no separate blades. You see a delicate gradation of tone as the surface of the ground rises and falls, but no detail can be seen.

Look nearer. Gradually tufts of grass become visible with shaded sides and vague little cast shadows—bumps merging one into the other—but still you cannot see individual blades. They become clearly visible only in the last few feet of the foreground, and even there, although you may attempt to model each one, they must be subordinated to the larger masses of which they are a part.

Always, in drawing, you must work from the large to the small, never vice versa !

The Sky.

In clouds you will find the most fleeting of all subjects. They will sometimes change completely while your eyes are turning down to your paper and up again. They must be drawn very swiftly and deliberately, or almost entirely from memory.

In spite of their evanescence they do sometimes appear quite solid and have light, half-tone, shade, and even cast shadows. Look, for example, at the exquisite modelling in a bank of cumulus clouds—particularly when the sun is shining—and at the shadows of low clouds which, on windy days, skim raggedly over the landscape.

Clouds take their place in a picture with the buildings and trees and all the other terrestrial things, and must, with them, be organised to produce a perfectly balanced, satisfactory design. They show recession just as clearly as the solid objects. Clouds near to the spectator appear larger than others exactly similar, at a greater distance, and not infrequently parallel lines of cloud appear to converge. Look, for example, at the so-called mackerel-back sky.

You should remember here, however, that horizontal clouds follow the curve of the earth and turn down behind the horizon; they do not go to a VP on a theoretical horizon at infinite distance. They could be drawn by taking them to a series of AVPs, each a little farther below the horizon than the last, but such a method would not normally be adopted. One should rely, rather, on careful observation.

Draw as many skies as possible from Nature; you can never have enough of them. The important clouds from the picture-making point of view are those which you can see without raising the head.

Finally, draw skies in pictures very delicately and lightly and keep them rather high in tone. Unless you do this they will tend to come in front of objects in the foreground and will seem to come down on your head.

Water and Reflections.

Sooner or later you will be tempted to introduce a pool or a pond into your drawing, and you will then require some understanding of reflections. These, like more tangible things, have to be analysed and reconstructed in a drawing.

I will explain first of all what a reflection is.

1. Some surfaces do not absorb light. Its rays, unable to penetrate, are reflected from them. They are called reflecting surfaces. A burnished metal plate is a perfect reflecting surface; a mirror is nearly perfect; and deep, still water is an imperfect reflecting surface— *i.e.*, most rays of light are reflected from it, but some pass through.

You will remember that light shining on an object is scattered from its surfaces, in all directions, in an infinite number of rays, and that one set of these rays conveys an image of the object to the eye. Suppose now that between ourselves and such an object there lies a horizontal mirror or a pond. A number of the visual rays which leave the object strike the reflecting surface and, unable to penetrate, are reflected once again. One set of these twice reflected rays converges on the eye, which thus receives two images of the object. We cannot see round corners, so one of these images appears to be in the pond—upside down!

In Fig. 42 I have drawn the complete reflection of our object—a barn, in this case—but I have shown dia-

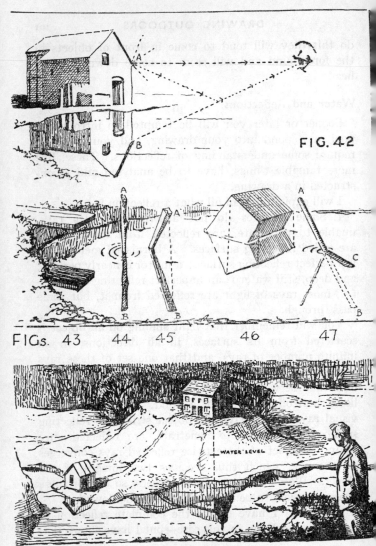

FIG. 42

FIGs. 43   44   45   46   47

FIG.

grammatically the two rays which convey to the spectator an image of point *A* and of its reflection, *B*, in the pond.

If a perpendicular is dropped from such a point *A* on to the reflecting surface and produced through it, point *B* will be on this produced line—as far away from the reflecting surface on one side as point *A* is on the other.

2. This fact enables us to place accurately the reflection of any given point. A perpendicular is dropped from it to the reflecting surface—to the surface of our pond, for example, or to water level. This perpendicular is produced through the reflecting surface until its length is doubled. If the reflecting surface is horizontal, the perpendicular will be in parallel perspective and it can be measured geometrically with dividers or with a ruler.

Fig. 44 is another very simple example of this construction. A stick stands vertically in a puddle. Its reflection is found by producing it to twice its length.

Fig. 45 shows the reflection of the stick when it is pushed obliquely into the puddle. The reflection of its top point is found first of all, and then joined to the point at which the stick actually enters the water.

In Fig. 46 a box has been dropped into the puddle. The reflections of all its corners are drawn and then joined up.

Notice that, in the reflection, we get an entirely new perspective of an object. We can see the top of the box itself, but in the reflection it is hidden. Sometimes planes which are not seen in the object are revealed in its reflection (Fig. 43).

Fig. 48 shows the reflections of two houses which are

built some distance away from the water's edge. The first stands on very low land, the second on a hill. In Figs. 45 and 46 the perpendiculars were taken to the surface of the water. In Fig. 48 *they are taken to water level—i.e.*, in Fig. 48 you have to imagine the water stretching on, *under* the hill.

There is a general levelling of tone in a reflection. Dark-shaded surfaces appear a little lighter, and light surfaces a little darker.

The reflections of objects in mirrors placed vertically or obliquely are constructed in exactly the same way. Important points are selected, and perpendiculars, drawn from them to the reflecting surface, are produced through it. These would be drawn to *V*Ps or *AV*Ps. Such lines are foreshortened, of course, and measurements along them cannot be made with dividers or ruler. They will be largely a matter for your own good judgment. Remember that the half of a foreshortened line which is nearer to you will always appear longer than the half which is farther away. Whenever you are in doubt about the probable appearance of a reflection, arrange a mirror and an object in the positions in which you want them, and see what actually does happen.

3. The surface of still water is not a perfect reflecting surface. A great many of the rays which meet it are repelled, as we have seen, but some go through it and are reflected to the eye from the bed of the pool. We may see, therefore, as well as reflections, things which lie below the surface of the water. If you wish to be very particular when you are drawing these, you will take into account the effects of refraction. Rays leav-

ing air and entering water, or vice versa, are bent slightly from their course, and the images which they convey are distorted. An object at the bottom of a pond will appear to be much nearer the surface than, in fact, it is. The pond will appear generally to be shallower. Because the bottom of the stick *AB* in Fig. 47 would appear to come nearer to the surface of the water, the stick would look bent, as *AC*. Experiment with a pencil and a basin of water to see that this is true. When water is clear, nearby objects throw no shadows on its surface, though shadows may be seen on the bottom. When the water is muddy and opaque, however, light is scattered from it and shadows show quite clearly on its surface.

Look carefully at water under varying conditions. In which parts of the surface of a muddy pond are the reflections most clearly seen—in the shadowed or the sunlit parts?

4. When the surface of still water is disturbed, reflections are broken up. So are the shadows on muddy water.

Each ripple and hollow, like a convex or a concave mirror, reflects something of what is above and on each side of it. You will find small reflections of bright sky invading and lightening shadowed places and encroaching upon the edges of houses and banks and trees. Reflected lines, which in still water are crisp and clear, will writhe and twist as they are picked up in the ever-changing surfaces of ripples.

You must study these things at first hand. Stand by a pond for ten minutes, considering the reflections. Then throw stones into it and observe what happens to its appearance as ripples spread in ever-widening concentric circles across its surface. Notice what happens when two such sets of ripples meet. Wait until the still surface is disturbed by a gust of wind and see how the reflections are affected by that. Stir mud from the bottom of the pond and study the shadows.

Look over Westminster Bridge, some night, at the reflections of lights along the Embankment. If the river were absolutely smooth, all these reflections would be small pin-points of light. Because the surface is troubled, however, they are picked up in all the ripples between you and each lamp, and stretch towards your feet in almost unbroken golden lines.

You might also consider the reflections of objects and of lights in wet pavements and roads.

The sea is, of course, a study in itself. One needs to understand and to love it before it can be painted with any sympathy. It lends itself, in any case, to painting rather than to drawing.

I, personally, find pools and mill-ponds and back-waters much more fascinating. Their beauty and subtlety can only be completely expressed in colour, but much can be done with a pencil.

Some draughtsmen use, for reflections in still water, pencil strokes which are all vertical; they draw consistently " down " their paper. This certainly gives a very watery effect. One seldom sees a country pond without a few ducks swimming on it or delving noisily in the mud at its edge. They can be made, in a picture, the excuse for all sorts of interesting ripples. The drawing of such moving things—of birds, animals and people—calls, however, for rather special knowledge, and is so important that we must give it a chapter to itself.

CHAPTER VII

FIGURES AND ANIMALS

I HAVE already urged you to study the structure of any static or semi-static object which you may be called upon to draw. It is even more important that you should do this when you take living, moving things for your models. In no branch of our subject does ignorance of structure produce such meaningless distortion and ugliness as in the drawing of animals and human figures. One frequently sees, on posters, bathing belles who are so malformed that they would be quite unable to walk, and I have seen, recently, in an advertisement, a drawing of a cow which looks like an inflated balloon, so little has its construction been understood.

I. The Human Figure.

When you are drawing men and women in their everyday attire you must not forget that there is a body underneath the clothes. Sometimes, when I am drawing a man or a woman in complicated clothes or in some difficult action, I indicate the nude figure first, very lightly, in line and shading, and draw the clothes on to it afterwards. Empty-looking trouser legs are thus avoided and there is less likelihood of my putting a deep fold where there should be solid bone and muscle. To make proper use of this method one needs, of course, to have had some experience of drawing from the nude. I strongly advise you to go, if it

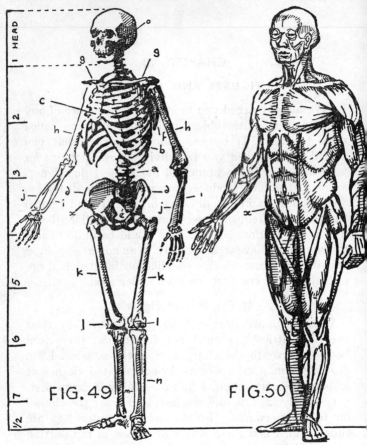

FIG. 49

FIG. 50

is at all possible, to a nude-life class at some Art School,* for it is true to say that, if you learn to draw

* Most Schools have evening classes for students who are unable to attend during the daytime.

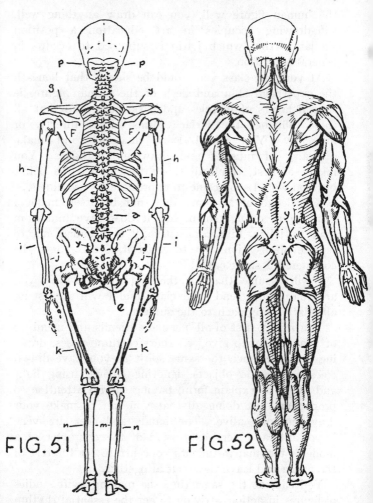

FIG.51   FIG.52

the human figure well, you can draw anything well. Life-drawing occupies in art education a position similar to that which Latin is supposed to occupy in general education.

At your life-class you would be shown that beneath the superficial skin and flesh of the human figure lie several layers of muscles and a skeleton, and that all these influence the surface forms, either directly or indirectly. You would learn anatomy and make diagrams of muscles and drawings of bones. You might, at first, think all this rather beside the point, but you would soon come to appreciate its usefulness.

Knowledge of anatomy does not by itself make a good figure draughtsman, but it does save him from many pitfalls. Like perspective, it is intended, not to replace observation, but to assist it. It is not to be considered a short cut.

I will assume that for the moment, however, you are unable to attend a life-class, and I will suggest an alternative approach to the subject.

You might, first of all, persuade friends and members of your family to give you short costume poses, drawing them in much the same spirit as you have drawn trees and static objects, ignoring colour, using light and shade to explain form, paying careful attention to proportion, but doing all that you can to make your drawings look alive. The hands and feet are very important, and very expressive of the character of a model : too many students concentrate on the rest of the figure and leave these out altogether.

You can, at the same time, be making swift studies of figures in action, striving to get the essential rhythm of their movement with a few well-chosen lines. Watch men working, driving wedges into the ground, swinging their hammers, digging and sweeping. Draw children running, skipping and climbing.

Then, when you have felt the need for it, study that part of this chapter which I have devoted to a very brief description of the anatomy of the human figure. You must do this in as practical a way as possible. When an art student goes to a lecture on anatomy, he sees the facts demonstrated on a living model. Muscles which are being studied may even be marked, on the skin, with lines and spots of paint. You may be able neither to see such demonstrations as these nor to work in a nude-life class, but you have always yourself to study, and you will go far to find a more patient model. When I mention some subcutaneous bone (one which lies immediately beneath the skin), see if you can find it on yourself; when I say that movement of a limb in a certain direction is limited, try the movement and see if it is true; when you are told that some action causes a change in the form of certain muscles, go through the action and, by keeping your hand on the muscles concerned or by watching them in a mirror, study the exact nature of the change.

The Human Skeleton.

You should know the shape, size, position and function of the most important bones, so I will deal with them in some detail, but you need not worry about their scientific names. I shall use such names only where there is no popular alternative.

Figs. 49 and 51 show front and back views of the

skeleton. You should study them carefully, preferably in conjunction with a real skeleton. You are almost certain to find one in your local museum.

It will be seen to consist of several distinct parts which, although covered by flesh and muscle, preserve their identity in the figure.

A. The Trunk, comprising the Backbone (*a*), the Thorax (*b*), a cage formed by twelve pairs of ribs all attached to the backbone, ten of them attached also to the Breastbone (*c*) in front;—the hip-bones or Pelvis (*d*), which is wedged on to the Sacrum (*e*), the bottom part of the backbone.

B. The Skull.

C. The Upper Extremities, each consisting of a Shoulder-blade (*f*), a Collar-bone (*g*), a bone of the upper arm, or Humerus (*h*), a forearm, a wrist and a hand. The forearm itself consists of two bones—the Ulna (*i*) and the Radius (*j*).

D. The Lower Extremities, each consisting of a thigh bone or Femur (*k*), a knee-cap (*l*), a leg, an ankle and a foot.

The leg consists of two bones—the Tibia (*m*) and the Fibula (*n*).

The Backbone.—This is a strong flexible column consisting of twenty-four jointed bones (vertebrae) arranged one on top of the other.

These increase in size from the top of the column to the bottom. Each of them is a rather squat, irregular cylinder with a bone ring behind it; there is a bony projection on each side of this ring and a spine at the back of it. The rings together make a long tube which contains and protects the spinal cord.

The first seven (cervical) vertebrae at the top of the column form the neck. On the uppermost of these (the Atlas) rests the head.

The next twelve are the dorsal vertebrae, and it is to these that the ribs are attached.

The next five (lumbar) vertebrae compose the " small " of the back.

There are five more vertebrae at the bottom of the column, but these are fused together and wedged immovably into the pelvis. This fused bone is called the sacrum. Below it, again, are several more tiny, rather shapeless, vertebrae which are all that is left of a tail.

The four distinct curves of the column are less apparent in the human figure than they are in the skeleton, for layers of muscle modify them considerably.

The backbone can be bent well forward and back again, slightly beyond the normal erect position. It can be moved to a lesser degree from side to side. There is also some rotation. Most of its movement takes place in the cervical and lumbar regions, movement of the dorsal vertebrae being slight because of their attachment to the ribs. Remember that the base of the column is fixed to the pelvis.

The spines of the vertebrae are subcutaneous, and when one bends forward they become very prominent. They are flanked, however, by large muscles, and in the erect figure their position is marked by a long furrow.

The sacrum, triangular in shape and curved, gives its form to the extreme bottom of the back.

The Thorax.—This need not detain us so long, for its

movement is very limited. The ribs curve downward from their articulations with the backbone, and all except the last two are joined to the breast-bone by elastic cartilage or gristle. This allows the sides of the thorax to expand in breathing.

The breast-bone is entirely subcutaneous, and its curved shape is clearly seen. The hollow which is found immediately above it is called the pit of the neck.

The cage of the ribs gives its form to the top part of the trunk and, although it is entirely covered by muscles, the individual ribs can sometimes be clearly seen— particularly, of course, in thin models.

The Pelvis or haunch-bones form a sort of basin which bears the weight of the trunk and transmits it to the legs. Each hip-bone consists of three irregular-shaped bones which meet in a hollow called the Acetabulum. Into this socket fits the round head of the thigh-bone. There is no movement between any of the bones of this pelvic girdle.

The pronounced "spines" at the back and front of the large bones are usually seen clearly in the nude model either as projections or, in "well-covered" people, as dimples (Figs. 49 and 50—x; Figs. 51 and 52—y).

The Skull.—You are, I expect, fairly familiar with the form of the skull. The cranium and the cheek, nose and jaw-bones determine the form and appearance of the head and face. Their shape and proportion differ in races and in individuals.

The head can be rocked and rotated very freely on the atlas; see for youself just how freely. The lower jaw-bone, is also capable of very free movement. The zygomatic ridges, Fig. 49 (o), running from the cheek-bones to the ears are very important to the artist; so are the mastoid processes, Fig. 51 (p), which point down and forward from behind the ears.

Notice the position of the ear in the side view of the head. It is practically midway between front and back.

The Shoulder-blades and the Collar-bones together form the two shoulder-girdles. Each collar-bone articulates with the top of the breast-bone : this is the girdle's only bone connection with the trunk. Movement with the breast-bone is quite free, but very slight.

The shoulder-blades are triangular and slightly curved to fit over the back of the thorax. On the back of each blade, pointing outwards and upwards, is a large ridge or spine which finally turns forward and terminates in a flat arch : you can feel it at the crest of your shoulder.

The collar-bone articulates with the end of this arch, on the inside of it. Below it, on the shoulder-blade, is the socket which receives the head of the humerus.

The whole length of the top of the collar-bone is sub-cutaneous, and it is seen very clearly in the nude figure, but the shoulder-blade, except for a thin line along the spine which may be seen as a furrow, is covered with muscles.

The Humerus is a long shaft with a round head which fits into the socket of the shoulder-blade to form a ball-and-socket joint whose movements are very free indeed. The arm can be raised to the level of the shoulder without disturbing the collar-bone and shoulder-blade, but when it is raised beyond that level—above one's head, for example—the end of the collar-bone rises with the socket, and the shoulder-blade rotates on the thorax.

The lower end of the humerus curves slightly forward, becomes flattened and terminates on each side in a prominence called a condyle, which is subcutaneous. Between these two condyles there are two surfaces. The inside one is not unlike part of a cotton reel; the outside one is part of a sphere. The first makes a joint with the top of the ulna of the fore-arm; the second is the ball upon which the head of the radius rotates.

The Ulna is a long bone situated on the inner side of the forearm. A deep notch just below the top of it works on the " cotton reel " which I have described to form a hinge-joint. Only simple flexion and extension are possible at such a joint.

The back of the top of this bone is the elbow or " funny "-bone. From here to the wrist a thin line of the bone is subcutaneous, marked by a furrow between the muscles along the whole length of the forearm.

The Radius is nearly as long as the ulna, and lies alongside it. It is so shaped and arranged that, while it must follow the flexion and extension of the arm, it can rotate at its articulation with the humerus and half cross the ulna. This movement is called pronation. The reverse movement is called supination.

The bone increases in size towards the wrist, where it articulates loosely with the small head of the ulna. The bones of the wrist are attached to the lower extremity of the radius, so, when the arm is pronated or supinated, the hand follows.

Hold your arm straight out in front of you, with the palm of your hand uppermost; that is the supine position. Now turn your palm towards the floor; that is the prone position.

The Wrist.—Curved and bony, the wrist articulates with the radius, and it can be flexed, extended, moved laterally and rotated. The head of the ulna shows as a prominent bump just behind the wrist—on the little-finger side.

The Hand.—Four long bones articulating one with another, and all with the bones of the wrist, form the back of the hand. The fifth, which belongs to the thumb, is capable of very free movement. The four bones end in the knuckles, which are ball-and-socket joints; the fifth, in the thumb, is more like a hinge.

Then come the fingers, consisting of three hinged bones, and the thumb, consisting of two. To the last bone in each series is attached the nail.

The upper extremities are lighter and looser than the lower extremities. They are designed for great freedom of movement. The lower limbs require, first of all, to be strong.

The Femur.—The thigh-bone is the longest in the whole body. Its head, which forms a ball-and-socket joint with the acetabulum—a hollow in the pelvis—is at the end of a short, strong neck which leaves the shaft, very near its top, at a slight angle. The two bones are, of course, much closer together at the knee than they are at the pelvis, so each of them inclines inwards as it descends. The outer side of the head of the shaft is sometimes discernible as a fulness in the model.

There is a great freedom of movement between this bone and the pelvis, but it cannot be extended back beyond the line of the trunk. Beware of breaking the hip-joint when you want to draw a man running or kicking a ball. If you want to get his leg right back, then his pelvis and trunk must lean forward accordingly.

The bottom of the shaft forms a sort of hinge-joint with the head of the tibia, the larger bone of the lower leg, and it has, towards the back on the inside and the outside, two bony projections which are clearly seen at the sides of the knee.

The Tibia, with the thin fibula, forms the lower leg. It lies on the inside, and gives the front of the leg its characteristic curve. Its shaft is three-sided, and one of these sides, facing forwards and inwards together with its front edge or crest, is entirely subcutaneous; it is commonly known as the shin-bone.

The knee can be flexed and extended and very slightly rotated, but there is no lateral movement. The lower extremity of the ulna is the subcutaneous prominence of the inner ankle-bone.

The Fibula.—Thin and almost entirely hidden by muscle, this bone lies on the outside of the tibia, parallel to it. It has no individual movement. Its lower extremity is the outer ankle-bone, situated rather lower than the inner one.

The Knee-cap, or Patella, is a small, triangular bone which rests on the front or on the bottom surface of the lower end of the femur, sliding over it as the knee is flexed and extended. It is entirely subcutaneous.

A knowledge of the character of the bones of the

knee is very useful—almost indispensable, indeed, to an artist, for its whole form is determined by them.

The Foot.—The first part of the foot is, like the wrist, composed of several irregular bones, and these extend quite half-way along it. The tallest of these bones articulates with the tibia and the fibula, allowing extension and flexion and a slight lateral movement. One other of them—the os calcis—is large and rather square, and extends back beyond the bones of the leg to form the heel.

From the front of these tarsal bones comes a series of " long " bones which closely resemble those in the hand. They decrease in length and size, and the last of them bears the toe-nail. The big toe has three such bones, the other toes four.

There is, as you know, less movement in these bones than there is in those of the hand. Many of the bones of the feet are, however, subcutaneous, and it is most important that the artist should understand them.

The general shape and size of all the bones mentioned here should be studied and memorised. You should study all the movable joints on your own person, so that, in drawing, you may never force the bones into impossible positions.

Proportion.

The proportions of the human figure are determined quite obviously by the relative size of the bones of the skeleton, so I will give you, here, some typical measurements.

Such measurements are always made in " heads "; a man is said to be seven and a half or eight heads high.

One head is the vertical distance from the top to the chin.

The collar-bone is rather less than one head long, so are the shoulder-blades and the breast-bone.

The humerus is one and a half heads long, and the radius is about one head long. The ulna is a trifle longer.

The femur is two heads long.

The tibia is a little more than one head and a half.

The crutch is, in a well-proportioned man, about half-way between the top of his head and the ground.

The knee-joint is half-way between the top of the femur and the ground.

The proportion of the bones differs in man and woman. A woman's frame is usually smaller and lighter than a man's, but her pelvis is much broader and shallower than his. He is broad at the shoulders and narrow in the pelvis. She is narrow at the shoulders and broad in the pelvis. The bones of her arms and legs are also relatively shorter than those of a man.

The Muscles.   (Refer to Figs. 50 and 52.)

The skeleton is covered with layers of muscles whose contractions, voluntary and involuntary, move the bones. I shall not deal with them in very great detail, for nearly all those which concern the artist are superficial and, given a little guidance, you will have no difficulty in locating and studying them for yourself.

Each muscle has two parts : one part which is fleshy and elastic, can be contracted and stretched; the other, connecting the muscle to its bones or to some other muscle, is called tendon, and is quite inelastic.

The form of both the fleshy and the tendinous parts varies in different muscles, but their purpose is always the same. The fleshy part contracts and shortens and pulls together the surfaces to which its tendinous extremities are attached.

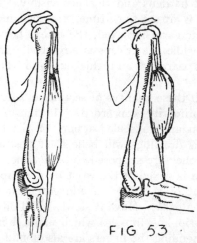

FIG 53

Take as an example the biceps muscle of the upper arm (Fig. 53). This is attached at its upper end to the shoulder-blade, and at its lower end to the radius near the elbow. When the fleshy part of the muscle contracts, in response to some message from the brain, its two insertions are drawn together. The shoulder-blade, being the more fixed, remains still, and the radius is drawn towards it—*i.e.*, the arm is flexed.

Muscles are usually found in opposing pairs, one flexing a joint, the other extending it again. The forearm, flexed by the biceps and by certain other deeper muscles, is straightened out again by the triceps, which, lying behind the upper arm, draws the elbow of the ulna towards the shoulder-blade and the top of the humerus.

When the fleshy part of a muscle contracts and shortens, it hardens and thickens visibly. The muscle opposing it is, at the same time, stretched and flattened. When the forearm is flexed, the biceps becomes round and hard, while the triceps is stretched. In extension the triceps hardens and thickens and the biceps is stretched.

It is with these changes of section and form that the artist is primarily concerned. He must understand construction and muscular action, or the form of the limbs in his drawings will belie their position and the movement they are supposed to be making.

The hand is flexed at the wrist by a group of muscles in the front of the forearm and extended by another group at the back. Move it slowly in all directions and watch the rippling muscles which make it move. The muscles extending the fingers are also found in the forearm, and their strong tendons are clearly visible on the back of the hand.

The large extensor and flexor muscles of the lower leg are found respectively in the front and back of the thigh. They also flex and extend the femur on the pelvis.

The muscles extending the foot lie at the back of the lower leg joining the top of the fibula and the bottom of the femur to the heel-bone. This group of muscles give the characteristic form to the calf, and the Achilles tendon which joins them to the heel is the strongest in the body. It is long and triangular, starting half-way down the leg and ending in a thick cord some three or four inches long. Extend your foot hard and study the form of this tendon and of these muscles.

The group of muscles which flexes the foot lies, as one would expect, in the front of the lower leg. Flex your foot and see how the muscles stand out.

Flexion and extension are not, of course, the only possible movements. There is rotation, abduction (drawing away from the middle line, as when the leg is raised sideways), adduction (drawing towards the middle line as when the leg is lowered again) and circumduction (making a circle—swinging one's arm round, for example).

In each action there are opposing groups of muscles. Consider the thick sterno-mastoid muscle of the neck which joins the mastoid process behind one's ear to the top of the breast-bone, and the inner third of the collarbone. When the left muscle comes into action the left mastoid process is drawn round until it is nearly over the pit of the neck, the head rotating on the atlas. The head is drawn back into position by the right-hand muscle.

The adductor group of the leg lies on the inside of the thigh, the abductor group on the outside.

The muscles which raise the arm lie above it—the large deltoid, for example; those which pull it down—the pectoral muscles and the latissimus dorsi lie below it in the chest and in the back.

Anything else which you need to know I am leaving you to teach yourself. Study Figs. 50 and 52 and try to locate the groups of muscles shown there, discovering their function and how their movements affect the surface form of the body.

Discover, for a start, which muscles supinate and pronate the forearm, where they originate, where they are inserted and how their form changes.

See which muscles raise the arm to shoulder level, and which muscles must then come into action to rotate the shoulder-blade and raise the arm above the head.

I have given you enough to be going on with, but if you wish to take the subject further, you will have no difficulty in finding books which treat it very exhaustively.

General Considerations.

There is a danger, when first you become conscious of bone and muscle, of making your nude and semi-nude figures look as though they have been skinned. You must avoid this danger by tempering your knowledge with sympathetic observation.

Bones and muscle are overlaid by layers of fat of varying thickness which modify their form considerably. This is particularly evident in the female figure.

When the head is held erect, the arms hung loosely at the sides and the weight of the body distributed equally to both feet, all its parts are symmetrical (Fig. 54). Viewed from the front, the medial line which runs from the pit of the neck, down the breast-bone, and between the abdominal muscles through the umbilicus, is straight and vertical.

Lines drawn from nipple to nipple, from shoulder to

shoulder and from knee to knee are horizontal. A line drawn between the dimples or prominences which mark the two front spines of the large hip-bone (the anterior superior iliac spines) is also horizontal.

The pit of the neck is vertically above a point midway between the two feet.

The figure is held in its erect position partly by balance and partly by muscular force exerted without conscious effort. Muscles in front of the body—in the neck, the abdomen, the thigh and the front of the lower leg—exert a downward pull and prevent the body falling backwards, while those at the back—in the neck and the spinal column, in the buttocks, the thigh and the calf—prevent it falling forwards.

Notice, by the way, that the neck has always a slight forward thrust; it is vertical only when the head is thrown back.

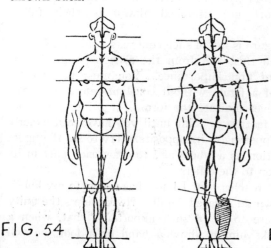

FIG. 54   FIG. 55.

When the weight of the body is thrown on to one foot, balance is maintained by a redistribution of the forms (Fig. 55). One side of the pelvis is thrust up, the other drops. In sympathy with this movement the shoulder on the side of the standing leg drops and the other one rises. The knees also take a different level. The medial line takes a strong curve, but the neck, in the front view, remains vertical.

The pit of the neck is found now to be vertically above the heel of the standing leg.

You will see that the bony forms of the skull, thorax and pelvis are, in their new positions, practically unchanged. The greatest changes have taken place in the soft parts between them. For example, the muscles between thorax and pelvis on the side of the standing leg are crushed into a small compass, while those on the other side, where pelvis and thorax have been drawn apart, are stretched almost to their fullest extent.

Every figure is full of such contrasts, some much more subtle than this, and from the artist's point of view they are of first importance. You must never draw one side of a figure without constant reference to the other. Never indicate the form of a group of muscles or of any feature or joint until you have seen exactly what is happening to its opposite. Try to see the figure and its action as a whole and to draw each part in its true relation to the others.

The best teacher that I know has never, to my knowledge, drawn an isolated detail. He considers the unity of the figure to be of such importance that, when a student asks him to draw a hand or a foot, he will

make a drawing of the complete pose and then elaborate
that particular part.

Clothes.

I have worked in life-classes over a period of many
years, yet I have never introduced a completely nude
figure into a picture. The training is of direct use, of
course, when one needs hands and bare feet or semi-
nude people such as boxers, natives and workmen stripped
to the waist, but anatomy and life-drawing are most
valuable because they enable the artist to draw quite
ordinary clothed figures with understanding and con-
viction.

The clothes themselves give plenty of scope for careful
observation and drawing, and their folds and creases
can be very expressive of the rhythmic action of the
figure.

Folds may be divided roughly into four kinds—those
which occur :

(1) in hanging materials;
(2) in material which is pulled;
(3) in material which falls into a heap, and
(4) in material which is crushed.

Hanging folds and folds which are caused by a pull
spring always from a point. Those which are caused
by heaping and crushing do not always keep the rules,
but you should be able to find good reasons for their
arrangement.

Flex your knee, or get somebody who is wearing
trousers to flex his for you. The folds which run from
the knee-cap down the front of the lower leg are hang-

ing folds; those behind the calf and in the bend at the back of the knee fall into category 3 or 4; the tight folds which spring from the crutch and lie, fan-shaped, along the inside of the thigh are pulled.

Crushed folds are seen very clearly in the bend of the sleeve when your arm is flexed.

Do not allow the shading on folds to destroy or contradict the modelling on the larger, more important, forms, and don't attempt to put in every little crease. The most significant and useful folds should be selected for inclusion in your drawing, and the rest ignored.

Portrait.

Expression and a good likeness are important in the drawing of a head, but they are not more important than its apparent solidity and the firm placing of the head on the neck and of the neck on the shoulders.

You should approach such a drawing very patiently, building it up just as you would a tree or a house or anything else, making all possible use of light and shade and of perspective, and ignoring colour completely. You are not concerned with the black or the gold of your model's hair, but with its form, its straightness or its waviness, and with the way in which it follows or builds up the form of his head.

The features may be supposed to lie on lines drawn round the form of the head (Fig. 56). One passing down the middle of the face bisects the forehead, the nose, the mouth and the chin. Measurements taken down this line show that the distance between the top of the forehead and the top of the nose is approximately equal to the distances between the top of the nose and the bottom, and between the top of the upper lip and the point of the chin. The mouth lies one-third of the way down the last of these divisions. Horizontal sections of the head taken through the eyes and the bottom of the nose include also the top and bottom of the ears. Another line bisecting the side of the head passes through the passage of the ear. These proportions vary in individuals, but the construction lines are useful when one

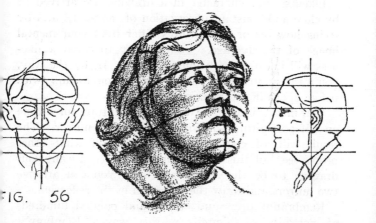

FIG. 56

is drawing a head above or below the eye-level or very much foreshortened.

You must know something of the skull and of the shape of the subcutaneous bones which we have already discussed. I have not found a study of all the muscles of the face to be of very great assistance in drawing it—close observation is much more use—but you should see how the surface form is affected by the strong Masseter muscle, which runs from the zygomatic arch to the

E—DRAW

angle and back half of the lower jaw-bone : you can feel it if you clench your teeth.

The muscles of the neck are also important, particularly the sterno-mastoid, which, with the top of the breastbone and the Adam's apple, forms the pit of the neck and gives form to the throat. Remember that the eye is a ball moving in a deep socket, and that the eyelid and the muscles surrounding it follow its form.

Likeness and character in a drawing are arrived at by close and constant observation of the model and by seeing how his or her features differ from your mental image of the average. Your ability to catch a likeness will improve with long practice. If, by the way, you want sympathetic criticism, you should think twice before appealing to your model for it.

You might, indeed, be wise to concentrate for a time on self portraiture—drawing yourself in a mirror. The result will, of course, be the reverse of what other people see, but this does not matter. If you want your drawing to be the right way round you can arrange two mirrors and draw the reflection of the reflection.

Rembrandt drew and etched and painted hundreds of portraits of himself in this way—" Rembrandt grimacing ", " Rembrandt with haggard eyes ", " Rembrandt in a fur cap ", etc., dressing up and disguising himself for the purpose.

2. Animals.

Man, like the horse, the cow, the dog and the cat, has four limbs, but, unlike these animals, he uses only two of them for walking. The power to carry and balance his whole weight on two legs came slowly to him, but it assured his emergence from the ranks of the less fortunate lower orders.

Fig. 58 shows that, in spite of this important difference, the structure of man and of these animals is not dissimilar. I have lettered some of the bones which correspond in all the skeletons.

Children drawing a horse or a cow from memory will

FIG.57

sometimes give the back leg a knee at *I* (see also Fig. 59). This is, of course, wrong. The child is right to expect a joint in the back leg corresponding to our knee, but it should be at *H*. The joint at *I* is, in reality, the heel of the animal.

In each diagram

        A is the shoulder-blade,
        B the pelvis,
        CD the bone of the upper arm or humerus,

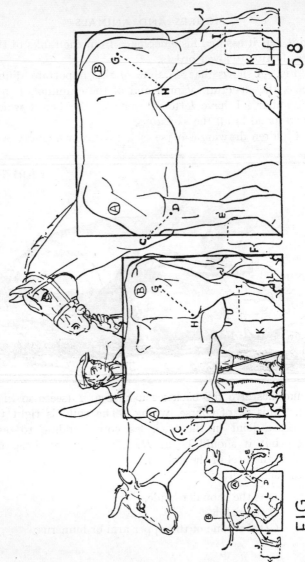

FIG. 58

> *D* the elbow,
> *E* the wrist,
> *F* the hand.

You have only to see a horse dragging a heavy cart uphill, gripping and clutching at the ground, to realise that *F* is its hand.

> *GH* is the thigh-bone or femur,
> *H* the knee,
> *I* the ankle,
> *J* the heel,
> *K* the foot, and
> *L* the toes

Four of its original five toes have, in the evolution of the horse, disappeared, and the middle one with its toe-nail now forms the hoof.

Look for these points when next you get sufficiently close to a horse or a cow. Go, if you can, to the Natural History Museum at South Kensington, where the skeletons of a man and of several animals are arranged in a group. You could learn a great deal from that group. You would see, for example, how the skeletons compare in height and size. A man can rest his elbow on the back of a cow, but the back of an average-sized cart-horse would be above his eye-level.

Fig. 58 will, however, give you some idea of this. See how the side-views fit into a square. The shoulder-blades of the man rest on the back of his thorax; those of the horse and the cow rest on its sides. Neither the horse nor the cow has a collar-bone, and the movements of the front legs are therefore very limited. The ulna

and the radius are, in both these animals, welded together, so there can be no pronation or supination of
the " forearm ".

The horse and the cow differ so greatly in form and
general appearance as a result of their selection and
breeding. The horse is an
active animal, bred either for
speed or strength, and its
muscles are fully developed and
powerful. The cow, on the
other hand, is bred solely for
the production of milk, and
great muscular development is

fig. 59.

unnecessary. The backbone, pelvis, shoulder-blades and
ribs show very clearly, particularly as there is little fat
in those quarters to modify the sharpness of the bones.

Bullocks and the draught-oxen which one still occa-
sionally sees are bred for flesh and muscle, and their
bones are not so prominent.

The muscles themselves differ in proportion from
those of the human figure and, consequently, they look
rather unfamiliar. In all other respects, however, in
composition and function, they are exactly the same.
They have tendinous insertions and a fleshy body which
contracts and stretches, flexing, extending or in some
other way moving the bones, and their movements
change the form and section of the parts in exactly
the same way.

The more you know of animal anatomy, the better
you will understand these changes of form, but your
knowledge is best obtained from careful first-hand
observation of moving animals, with occasional reference,

perhaps, to a book of diagrams. You may find that your Public Library has books such as these, or that the librarian is willing to obtain one for you, but book-learning alone is not enough. If you are really to master the subject you must *draw* and keep on drawing.

Studies of domestic animals and birds, horses, cows, pigs, sheep, goats, chickens, ducks, etc., can be made most conveniently in and about the farmyard, and studies of dogs and cats in the house. It is also impossible to make a finished drawing of any of them at one sitting, because they are so restless. One has usually to make a great many careful studies of details, and several swift drawings of complete poses, and then to combine and adjust all these at leisure, aided perhaps by snapshots and cuttings from farming weeklies. I shall have more to say about the use of photographs in the next chapter.

The details are best studied from living animals in the field, the stable or the milking-shed, but use may sometimes be made of such things as hoofs, sheep's-heads and pigs'-trotters obtained from the butcher's shop.

The drawings of complete poses may be made in line with as much significant shading as time permits. Drawing several different views of an animal—back, front, side and three-quarter views—will help you to understand its form. You should indicate any girth or strap which helps to show a section. If you intend to use horses in your pictures you should examine and memorise the details of the various types of harness that are used.

You must also make a great many action studies of

animals. They should be made, like your drawings of human figures, with a few, well-chosen, very expressive lines, and they should be as complete as possible. They demand great concentration on the part of the artist, a keen eye, a good memory and no little patience. You should attempt to draw horses walking, trotting, galloping and jumping, and to represent the character-istic movements of other animals. You have probably noticed that cows struggle to their feet from a lying position hindquarters first. Snapshots can be helpful in studying these movements, and excellent close-ups of animals in action are sometimes to be seen at the Cinema. The Circus also gives one an opportunity of seeing very fine horses in action.

When, for some reason or another, an animal seems likely to remain still for a time, you should seize the opportunity and make a complete and detailed drawing. It may be tethered securely, or it may be lame and disinclined to move very far. When a delivery van stands outside a house for a long while and the horse is quiet, you could draw not only the horse, but the van as well, and perhaps make a careful study of the harness. You may even find a horse in a field, sleeping on its legs, and be able, without disturbing it, to walk quite close.

Cows probably give one more opportunities of this kind than horses. They lie down for hours on end chewing the cud, or they graze slowly from one end of a field to the other, so that you are able to walk beside one, very quietly, and draw her as she falls, time and again, into the position you require. You must beware, when you are doing this, of making contradictions of perspective and of putting something of two positions into one drawing.

You must always be ready to seize a good opportunity when it offers itself. When you are in the middle of a study of a tree or a barn, and you suddenly notice a cow or a pig or a duck in some position which it seems likely to maintain, turn your attention to it at once. The barn and the tree will be there in the same position next day. The animal will most certainly not!

It is usually necessary to stand and to walk about when you are drawing animals outdoors, so your equipment, including the board or portfolio (*see* Chapter 1), should be as light as possible.

A certain amount of useful work can be done from stuffed specimens in museums, but you will not very often find domestic animals there.

I was able once to draw a number of stuffed ducks and chickens in a museum, and these, with some action studies of real birds which I made later in a farmyard, have been most useful.

White plaster casts of animals can also be very useful. You will sometimes find these in a museum, too, but they can be bought fairly reasonably. A cast of a horse, waxed and highly polished, helps one to understand and place the shine on a glossy coat, but this, though useful to the painter, is seldom necessary in a drawing.

Wild and foreign animals can also be studied in museums and from photographs, but they should first be seen and drawn in the flesh. Museum specimens prepared and mounted by a good taxidermist are very lifelike and make excellent models, but in the very best of them the underlying structure, so important to the artist, is artificial. You would be wise to get your first impressions and make your first drawings at a Zoo.

3. Animals and Figures in Pictures.

If a picture is to be a figure composition—one in which the figures and animals are of most importance—they will, as a rule, occupy the foreground and be made quite large.

They must, like trees or buildings (Chapter IV), be placed securely on the ground, some nearer to us than others, some partly obscuring others from our sight, and they should all seem able to move from the position in which we see them. Watch the perspective of your animals, particularly if they are foreshortened, and see that all four feet are correctly placed. A rectangle drawn on the ground in the required perspective—one corner for each foot—may be useful as a guide, especially when several animals are standing in a group.

When you are drawing a large number of cows or sheep it is not necessary to make a portrait of each one ; try rather to generalise—to seize the characteristics of the whole herd or flock.

A crowd of people needs to be designed not in terms of single figures, but in groups—in shapes and masses and patterns of light and shade made by several people together. A crowd does break naturally into such groups, talking, arguing or gaping at something of interest, so if you keep your eyes open you will find plenty of excuses for grouping in your pictures.

Care should be taken that the spectator's eye is led easily to the centre of interest, and not sent all over the picture searching for it. If, for example, you desire to call attention to a brawl in a market-place, the action should be confined to the three or four people concerned, and the rest of the crowd be kept fairly still. You might even arrange for sunlight to fall upon this one group and shadow upon all the others. Lines of roofs and cobbles converging in perspective, and the limbs and glances of passers-by, may also help to lead the eye in the right direction.

Animals and people will, as a rule, be introduced into your work last of all, from memory or from notes and studies made elsewhere. You will have to develop and rely a great deal on your memory, for, even when you have a good study, it will need putting naturally into its new context; it may need turning right round, or it may be so incomplete, your subject having bolted half-way through, perhaps, that it can be no more than a reminder. So we turn now to a consideration of your difficulties in drawing without a model.

CHAPTER VIII

DRAWING FROM MEMORY

THERE are three ways of making a drawing from memory:

(1) The subject, thoroughly understood from previous examination and analysis, is reconstructed in the drawing.

(2) The drawing is made from a mental image of the subject which can be called before the mind's eye time after time.

(3) In the third and best method these two are combined. A concern with merely superficial things which may result from the second method is prevented by a sound understanding of structure, while the ability to visualise one's subject gives the drawing a certain breadth and unity and brings to mind a wealth of significant detail which might otherwise be forgotten.

The first method is based, of course, on knowledge. The more you know of your subject, the better you can draw it. The man who rides, cleans and repairs a bicycle is more familiar with its construction than another man who is not a cyclist, and he should be able to draw it better from memory.

You must understand the function of anything you draw. If any of its parts are movable you should see how they move and to what purpose. You must be able

FIG.60

to make a drawing which looks as though it would work.

It is not, as a rule, much use making an "impression" of a chair or a mangle; your drawing should be so self-explanatory that a craftsman might, with no other guide, construct the object represented.

When you are able to make a special study of the object to be drawn, you should approach it just as though you intend making a sight-drawing, comparing height and width, noticing the apparent direction and length of the main lines, using your pencil to compare their inclination with the vertical and horizontal, using all the aids outlined in previous chapters, but committing your observations to memory instead of to paper.

The drawing itself will be built up or reconstructed gradually, with due regard to perspective, light and shade and, in the case of figures and animals, anatomy. If you thoroughly understand the construction of your subject, you will be able to draw it in any other position. Everything that has been said, in earlier chapters, of drawing things from sight, will apply equally when you are drawing them from memory.

One usually resorts to memory-drawing, however, when an ordinary study of the subject cannot be made; when, for example, a windmill and a barge are required in an illustration and neither a canal nor the country is within easy reach. You should, therefore, take an interest in the structure and appearance of anything which seems even remotely likely to be of use in the future, examining it thoroughly, and memorising as much of it as you can. A small pocket sketch-book for drawn and written notes should be carried wherever you go.

The second method is one to which most artists resort more or less unconsciously, but it has certain obvious virtues which commend it to the educationalist, and it has been singled out recently for a great deal of attention.

Something which you see appeals to you. It may be anything—a tree, a boat, a whole landscape; let us suppose that it is a stationary farm wagon. You look fixedly at it, noticing all its proportions, the position of its parts, its fine, sturdy wheels, its shafts and all its details. You see how the powdery blue of the body contrasts with the rather peculiar pink of the wheels, how in places it has become almost white, and how in others some load has stained it to a deep yellowish-green. You are aware of a mass of green leaves behind it all, a blur of red tiles, of dusty white ground with a thin, clear shadow of wheels and spokes and shafts upon it. You contemplate rather than study these things. Then you turn about and close your eyes to find that a fairly clear impression of all that you have seen remains with you. Some parts are still very vague, however, so you turn once more to the cart, and you continue to do so until you are satisfied that your visual image is complete.

Later on, at home, you sit down to make a picture. You close your eyes and visualise the scene once more. It may at first be very indistinct, but concentration brings it all quite clearly before you. By repeatedly closing your eyes and examining this image you will be able to complete a drawing—copying what remains of the scene in your mind's eye.

You will see there things of which you were quite unconscious at the time, while other, for the most part unessential details will completely escape you. The mind makes its own selection of what it considers important in your scene. It also offers suggestions for the arrangement of your picture. You may find, when you close your eyes, that strange things are happening to the setting of your cart. Trees, walls, people, pigs, all sorts of things which you have seen at other times and in other places stray into your mental picture and, if you are sensitive to suggestions, as an artist should be, some of these will be introduced into your drawing.

Very often they are just what it needs.

Complete pictures sometimes flash across the " inward eye " in this way. At certain times—just between sleeping and waking, for example—the stored-up contents of the subconscious mind—observations, facts, visual impressions and all manner of half-formed ideas—pass into the conscious mind, mysteriously digested and recombined into new quite clear and very personal images.

Because this second method of drawing helps to release such mental conceptions, children in more enlightened schools are encouraged to use it, and to find their " Imaginative " pictures in the mind's eye.

The ability to visualise is particularly useful when one is trying to draw moving animals and people. A galloping horse defies analysis, except by a slow-motion camera, but it is possible to seize and reproduce a mental image of one stage of its progress. The prehistoric cave-drawings of animals must have been made in this way, and they suggest that the primitive hunter-artist possessed keen vision and really remarkable powers of observation.

The quality of the mental image varies enormously in

different people, but its clarity and usefulness can be increased with systematic practice. You should make a habit of setting yourself subjects which must be visualised. When you have been to the theatre or to the pictures you should attempt to reproduce a scene which has particularly impressed you. Try also to draw rooms in boarding-houses and hotels in which you have stayed, or, better still, of houses from which you have moved—things which exist no longer, except in your memory.

The third method—a combination of these two—is the best, for reasons which I have already explained and which you will now understand.

The Compilation and Use of a Reference File.

Illustrators, commercial artists, and a great many painters collect cuttings and photographs, mount and index them carefully and refer to them when knowledge and memory fail.

The illustrator, usually a very busy man, has little time to go into the country or to the museum making studies, and he has to rely almost entirely on his collection of references. His needs seem to be quite limitless. One minute a photograph of Vesuvius may be required, the next an Indian carpet or the garb of a Billingsgate porter. Anything and everything which might, on some future occasion, be useful goes into his file.

The painter's work usually covers a more limited field of his own choosing, and his collection of references is not so large. It contains, as a rule, photographs of things which he may need but which are, for some reason, not easily accessible to him—of things which are not easily studied from life. There may be, for example, animals and figures in action, boats in full sail, birds in flight, circus pictures, clouds and trees. A man's interests are reflected pretty faithfully in the contents of his reference file.

The most useful photographs are those which you take yourself. When I go out painting or drawing I take with me a small box Brownie which I have had for some fifteen years. It does not add much weight to my load, but it has given me some invaluable reference. See always that the light really shows up the form of your subject; get some good half-tones and shadows into it. Too many amateur photographers arrange themselves so that the sun shines from directly behind them, and, as a result, their prints lack all sense of relief.

Friends sometimes take " snaps " which look very useful, and they are usually willing to lend the negative for a day or two.

Monthly magazines and weekly papers also provide good material, but newspaper cuttings are not as a rule satisfactory, very quickly turning yellow and becoming useless for reference. Excellent pictures frequently appear in the daily papers, however, and if you are sufficiently enamoured of any one to spend a few shillings, prints from the original negative can be obtained from the head office of the newspaper.

When first I began collecting references, I made the common mistake of pasting them into a scrapbook, which was very soon filled. They are best pasted on to loose sheets of stout, brown or grey paper and stood upright in a drawer or box. Sheets of card slightly taller than the papers should be arranged between them, at intervals, to divide the reference into sections. At the top of each card should be printed the contents of the section behind it—CIRCUS, FAIRS, TREES, etc. I shall not attempt to suggest a list of titles with which to begin, for that is a very personal matter. So long as loose sheets are used, new sections can be added and existing ones sub-divided at will, and as your collection increases in size, it can spread into a second and perhaps even a third drawer. Remember, however, that quantity is to be sought less than quality and usefulness.

One's own drawings and studies may also be kept, under their appropriate headings, in the reference file.

All references for one subject should, as nearly as possible, be kept together. When, for example, you pull out the sheets in a section marked DOGS, you should find there all the dogs you have, and nothing but dogs. This facilitates use of the file, reducing the number of sheets which have to be handled.

When one photograph contains several different objects—all good references—it should be filed in the section devoted to one of them and a note made of it in each of the sections devoted to the others.

The size of the sheets of paper you use will depend on the drawer or box in which you intend to keep them, but a quarter imperial sheet—15″ × 11″—is useful.

I advised you, at the end of Chapter 1, not to use flat copies. This chapter may seem to contradict that, so it must be emphasised that references are not to be copied, or even, necessarily, adapted, but used rather as a source of information and as a stimulus to the memory.

A photograph is very little help to anyone who cannot already draw quite well; it may even mislead him rather

badly.   A slavish copy of one will always betray itself
as such, for the camera, unlike the artist, cannot select
and reject.   It confuses dark colours with shade and
shadows, and too often it loses the cool blue half-tones
altogether.   Begin collecting your reference at once, but
don't attempt to use it until you know exactly what you
want from it and what you can expect it to give you.

CHAPTER IX

SOME OTHER MEDIA

THE term " drawing " is not confined to work which is produced with a lead pencil. A study made in pen and ink is a Pen Drawing; one consisting of transparent washes of grey, brown or some other colour, on a pen-and-ink foundation, is a Pen-and-Wash Drawing. A Wash Drawing is made with unfixed Indian ink, ivory black or process black, or with pencil and any water-colour.

All these methods of making a drawing fall within the scope of this book, but before I consider them in detail I must mention some more materials which are not, however, in use or effect, very different from those which you have already met. I am unable to quote prices of any materials because these are liable to fluctuation, but you can discover how much they cost at the present moment by obtaining catalogues from the nearest dealer in artists' materials, or direct from the manufacturers, whose names and addresses you will find in a telephone directory.

Charcoal.—Charcoal drawings are, as a rule, larger and coarser than pencil drawings. They are best made at an easel. Venetian or a good Vine charcoal should be used on Ingres or Michallet paper—white, cream or light grey. Grey sugar-paper is also quite satisfactory. The charcoal may be used in a metal holder—usually called a portcrayon.

Carbon Pencils.—These, like ordinary lead pencils, are graded, but they are all more intensely black, and they give a smooth, velvety line which is without shine. They should be used boldly and deliberately, on a paper which has a slight " tooth ".

The black crayon may be used alone on white, cream or light grey paper. It may also be used in conjunction with the white crayon on a mid-grey paper. In this case the black is used to give shade, shadow and dark half-tones; the black and white together to give light half-tones; and the white alone to heighten the lights. The grey of the paper should also be allowed to play its part in the half-tones.

The sanguine crayon is not so popular now as it was some years ago. It is red, of course, dull, and rather orange, and it is best used on a cream or light fawn paper. Studies of figures and heads look well in sanguine, but the colour is very flattering to a drawing, hiding a " multitude of sins ", and it should be avoided until you are very sure of yourself—and very critical.

Conté Pencils.—Conté crayon is also sold in pencil form. The pencils are made of cedar, polished or un-polished, and stamped " Conté à Paris ". They are, in every respect, the same as the crayons, but they have the advantage of being less fragile.

Fixative.—All charcoal, chalk and carbon pencil drawings are liable to smudge very badly, and they should be fixed as soon as they are completed. Place an atomiser, made of metal or glass, in a bottle of fixative, direct it towards your drawing and blow through it.

The fixative is ejected in a fine spray, which spreads all over the surface of the paper and then evaporates very quickly, leaving a thin film of shellac to protect the drawing.

Do not put the atomiser too near the drawing, and see that no large spots of fixative are blown on to it. The drawing should be kept flat during this operation.

Pen Drawing.—A pen with a nib, or nibs, to your own liking (Chapter 1), a bottle of smooth, fixed Indian ink and some paper or board with a hard, smooth surface are required for pen drawing. Higgins' American Indian Ink is excellent and, if a drawing is intended for reproduction, smooth Bristol board provides the best surface on which to work.

Be careful to keep your nib clean, for even the best ink will very soon clog it up.

It is necessary, when making a pen-drawing, to know exactly what you are going to do before you actually begin, so you should make a number of preparatory drawings in pencil, and perhaps a trial shot in ink as well. Finally, a careful pencil-drawing should be made on the board, or traced on to it from the best of your trials. It must be fairly complete, and all the shaded parts, half-tones and shadows should be indicated lightly. Then, on this foundation, in which all constructional difficulties have been overcome, you should get to work with the pen, using the pencil-shading as a guide to the arrangement and the strength of your pen-shading.

You should concentrate at first on the shaded areas, leaving the lights until you are in a better position to decide what can safely be done with them. Your darkest darks can be put in with a brush, for a certain amount of pure black is required in practically every drawing to give it a sparkle.

You can obtain any tone between these extremes of black and white by varying the thickness of your pen-strokes and their distance apart. The texture of the surfaces with which you are dealing may be shown at the same time by the way in which you apply the pen-strokes. You can shade in parallel straight lines—vertical, horizontal or inclined : in sets of parallel lines which cross one another at an angle, leaving a series of white dots between them which gradually decrease in size as new sets of lines are added to darken the area (cross hatching) ; in short " ticks ", which are drawn together or farther apart, as you require, to darken or lighten the tone; in dots; in little, wriggly lines. Leaves, hair, patterned clothes, etc., will suggest their own treatment, but remember that, except in special circumstances, texture must be kept subservient to light and shade.

When your drawing is nearing completion and all the pen-work which you have put into it is quite dry, rub out the pencil foundation. You may find yourself left with a drawing which is much lighter and thinner than you supposed, but don't be discouraged. Work right across the whole thing again, adding accents of dark where necessary, adjusting and finishing it as you go.

A pen drawing must consist quite frankly of lines, but do not rely overmuch on outline. Keep this very simple and rather severe, and concentrate on the forms which it encloses.

When you feel that you can work with sufficient assurance you might attempt some pen-drawing from life, dispensing with the preliminary pencil drawing. Never allow yourself to scribble; be very deliberate, and don't waste a single line. A fountain pen would be very useful for outdoor work, but Indian Ink clogs the ordinary type, and nobody has, to my knowledge, produced one specially for our purpose.

See Figs. 2–7, 9, 41–48, 57 and 58, all of which are pen drawings.

Tracing.—I have recently mentioned tracing. A drawing may be quickly and accurately transferred from one surface to another by this method. A piece of transparent paper is held or pinned firmly over the original and the main lines of the drawing are traced on to it. It is then turned over, and the lines, which show clearly on the reverse side, are worked over carefully with a soft pencil. The tracing is then placed in position right way round again, on the plain paper or board, and the lines are worked over once more—this time with a fairly hard pencil. The soft lead on the reverse side is pushed on to the surface below, and when the tracing-paper is removed a clear impression of the drawing remains. It is often quite enough to press the impression through with the edge of the thumb to save the third pencilling, or a spoon edge is most effective.

Dry Brushwork.—Useful broken textures may sometimes be introduced into a drawing with a brush which is almost devoid of ink or colour. When it is dragged over the paper, the colour catches on the rough surface, but fails to get into the hollows. To be really successful this must be done very skilfully, and it requires practice.

Splatter Work.—It is necessary sometimes—especially in advertising work—to shade one's paper evenly from white to black, or from white into a colour. This would be done in a studio by spraying liquid paint through an air brush, but a similar effect can be obtained at home with far less expensive materials.

A stencil brush or a small cube cut from a fine rubber sponge, dipped into paint of a suitable consistency, worked out until nearly dry on a piece of scrap paper and then dabbed lightly over a surface, will give the desired effect.

Alternatively, you might fill an old tooth-brush with ink or colour, point the head towards the surface which you wish to splatter, and send a fine spray of colour on to it by drawing the blade of a knife along the tops of the bristles—towards yourself. Surfaces which are not to be splattered should be protected with small sheets of paper. If you wish to shade away from an edge—round a head, for example, or away from the outline of a tree—a paper mask should be cut to the required shape and held in position, while you stencil or splatter against it.

Spraying and masking are used a great deal in posters.

Wash-Drawing.—Any water-colour paper is suitable for wash-drawing. Heavy cartridge paper may also be used, but it is not so satisfactory. These papers should, if possible, be stretched (Chapter 1). Water-colour boards can be obtained ready prepared, however, and these are particularly useful when work is intended for reproduction.

" Wash-drawing " means, to most painters, a study in pencil or ink, in which half-tones, shades and shadows are replaced or reinforced by transparent washes of water-colour. There is no need to describe the making of such a drawing in detail because you already know, from preceding chapters, how to set about it. The preliminary drawing need not, of course, be quite complete in itself; much of the required effect can safely be left to the washes of colour. These will vary in depth and transparency according to the amount of water which is put into them. Black water-colour can be used pure or it can be reduced to the palest grey and to an infinite number of tones between these two extremes. Sepia is another very suitable colour, and I have seen drawings in various shades of grey green, in a variety of browns and in blue.

Artists' water-colours, in tubes, should be used, mixed in china or enamelled palettes.

It is useful to have two large brushes, one for the colour and the other full of clean water to blend washes one into another and to soften edges where necessary. The paper may conveniently be sponged over with clean water and allowed to dry a little before you begin painting. If this is done, your first washes will flow very readily and be rather soft at the edges. Areas which need to be sharp of edge, also strong accents of shade, can be added last of all, when the paper has almost dried.

Strong, rather " rich " wash-drawings are made on a foundation of carbon pencil. Use may be made of the fact that pencil takes better on paper which has received a wash of colour than it does on untouched paper.

An illustrator's wash-drawing is more likely to be made with pure washes of process black or Higgins unfixed Indian Ink combined sometimes with pen-work. He also uses body-colour—process black and process white combined. It is not advisable to use wash and body-colour together. Pencil is used, of course, in building up the illustration, but it plays no part in the finished drawing.

Scraper Board and the White Line.—Before photo process engraving was introduced, the illustrations in books and journals were printed from wood blocks. The artist made his drawing on a plank or on the end-grain of a block of boxwood. An engraver was then employed to cut away the untouched surface, so that the drawing was left in relief. Ink was applied to it with a roller, and a sheet of paper was pressed on to it. If the engraver was really skilful, a facsimile of the drawing appeared in reverse on the paper when it was removed.

Pieces of plank cut with chisels, gouges and a knife are woodcuts; boxwood blocks engraved with burins or gravers are wood engravings.

These illustrations were, quite frankly, clever reproductions and nothing more, but Thomas Bewick (1735–1828), who made the *History of Quadrupeds*, etc., designed and engraved his own blocks in a truly creative way. Instead of making a drawing on the block and then cutting round it, he blacked the whole surface and built up his picture in cuts—in white lines, white ticks, and white cross hatching. His white line method is used by nearly all wood engravers today.

You will see examples of it in Figs. 60 and 64, but you will be surprised to learn that these are not wood engravings at all, but drawings made on scraper board.

Scraper-board drawings, reproduced by the line process, are widely used for illustration in books and advertisements, and when you see something in a newspaper which looks like a wood engraving, you may be pretty certain that it is an imitation of one—made on scraper board.

The board has a soft chalk surface, covered with a thin film of black ink. This ink can be scratched away with any sharp instrument to disclose the white surface below. White lines, white cross hatching, white dots and ticks can all be made, just as they are in wood engraving. Making a drawing on scraper board is rather like drawing on a blackboard with white chalk; instead of putting in shade and shadows, as you would with a pencil on white paper, you take out the lights. A knowledge of form and of construction is therefore as necessary here as in ordinary drawing, and textures should as a rule be kept subservient to light and shade. You should be equally cautious in using outlines. It is fatal to put a white line round everything, but beginners nearly always make this mistake.

British Pens, Ltd., make a series of scraper-board tools, of which numbers 1 and 2 are the most useful. Other sharp instruments may also be used for this purpose—pen-knives, vaccination nibs, etc.

It is usual to make a fairly complete drawing of one's subject on cartridge paper. This is then traced, but, instead of pencilling on the reverse side of the tracing, you place a piece of red transfer paper between it and the board. When the lines of the drawing are worked over with a hard pencil they are transferred to the black surface in red, which shows up very clearly. These red lines should be pencilled in at once—very lightly, so as not to scratch the board—or they will be rubbed off by the hand. The actual scraping may now be commenced.

Mistakes can be corrected with Indian ink, but you should use it as little as possible for the surface is easily spoiled. A combination, in one drawing, of pen-lines and white scraped lines, is not unusual.

Scraper board lends itself to almost indistinguishable imitation of wood engraving, but it has possibilities of its own, and these should be exploited. It has, for example, a greater fluency than wood engraving. Long, sinuous lines, varied in thickness along their length, can be made on scraper board fairly easily. That there is a danger in this very fluency goes without saying, and your approach must be very deliberate and disciplined.

Scraper boards can be bought white and brushed evenly to blackness, with fixed Indian ink, at home. They can also be bought ready blacked for use, but I have always found the surface of this variety rather tough and un-sympathetic.

Patterned scraper boards for use in advertisement drawing are made to obviate certain mechanical processes of reproduction. There is one with white ridges and fine black lines crossing them, known as No. 7; another with large ridges and black lines running between them (No. 8a) (Figs. 31, 39 and 40). These and many other prepared surfaces can be obtained from Clifford Milburn or Lechertier Barbe. Scraping will reduce areas to pure white; the addition of Indian ink will make solid black and any number of half-tones can be obtained.

If you are interested in any of these methods and you wish to acquire a good technique, you might study the work of their more able exponents. You must not copy them or allow yourself to be unduly influenced, but you should always take a lively interest in what other people are doing.

Watch the daily papers, commercial journals, weekly and monthly magazines, and cut out any good illustrations and advertisements that you find. Arrange them in your reference file under the names of the artists, or under the various methods.

CHAPTER X

BIAS

I. Further Advice for the Amateur.

IT should not take you very long to read and understand the whole of this book, but you will not learn its lesson or make any branch of the subject really your own without years of actual drawing. You will need great patience. You will need, also, to be a severe critic of your own work, though not a pessimistic one. You must never allow apparent failure to discourage you.

Had I attempted to make your task appear easy, I should have misled you. I could, for example, have given you a book of hints and recipes—" How to draw a cat in three easy stages "—but that sort of thing gets nobody anywhere. It is, as I hope you have already decided, an essentially wrong approach.

You may think, however, that I stress the technical and intellectual aspects of drawing too much, and the emotional aspect too little. I do this because I feel that these alone can be learned from a book or, for that matter, from any source. If you could be taught how to put emotion and expression into your drawing, you would become a mere sounding-board and your work an echo of your teacher's personality. If you really have something to say—if you are an " artist " as opposed to a mere painter or draughtsman—it will soon become apparent without any conscious effort on your part.

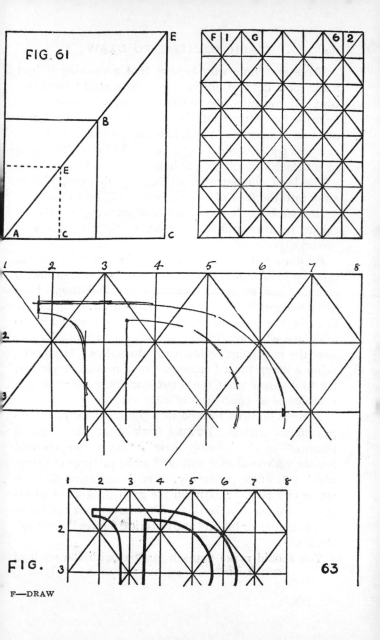

FIG. 61

FIG. 62

F I G

6 2

FIG. 63

F—DRAW

There are those who believe that a drawing is best made for a definite purpose—*e.g.*, as a study for a picture. If you subscribe to this opinion, your studies can be made for compositions in pencil, pencil and wash, pen and ink, scraper board and, later on, for lino-cuts, woodcuts and perhaps wood engravings. These crafts can all be satisfactorily followed at home.

The keen amateur will doubtless wish eventually to stray into the field of colour, and he will find that there again sound drawing is at the root of everything. Water-colour, tempera and oil-paint are media with which he should experiment.

He must not be lured away by the apparent ease of other people's methods or by the lawlessness which characterises so much contemporary painting. Ease and freedom, if they are to be worth anything at all, must be the outcome of sound training. Students too often ape what are, in fact, a mature artist's faults and miss the real point of his work altogether. If you develop a liking for a " manner " or a particular picture, try to discover what the artist was doing when he was your age or at your stage of his development.

There is no need for you to adopt other people's subject-matter either. Do not seek after the " grand manner " or the " heroic style ". Try to see life and Nature with your own eyes and make pictures of things which you know personally, even though they do seem rather ordinary. Nearly all the great masters of painting have done exactly this. They have even been content to give their biblical and historical figures " modern " clothes.

You should make yourself familiar with the work of

such painters and with the work of modern artists to be found both in public galleries and in private collections.

—and for the Embryo Commercial Artist.

Now, for the first time, I will pay particular attention to the reader who has what, for want of a better phrase, I will call a commercial bias.

I have avoided doing so before because no student should even think of specialising until he is able to *draw* really well. Those who do achieve a measure of success in the field of commercial or industrial art without such ability, do so because their work possesses a certain inevitable *naiveté*—a gaucherie which can be very attractive and which happens, at the present moment, to be very popular. When, however, fashion changes, as it very frequently does, such people have no foundation on which to build another style and their market passes to some new nine-day wonder.

Moreover, applied art is not essentially different from other forms of art, and it should not be taught as though it were. It is always a reflection of current or slightly earlier work in the fine arts. The modern poster as we know it would never have existed had it not been for experiments made in painting by Picasso and his followers in England and on the Continent.

Indeed, nearly all the book-jackets, illustrations, posters and package designs which really count for anything have been the work of men and women who received their training as painters, sculptors or engravers. A sound foundation of drawing is not merely an advantage; it is essential if work of lasting merit is to be produced.

When, however, with the necessary mastery of drawing, one does turn to work of this kind, certain adjustments in both technique and design are seen to be necessary.

2. Drawing for Reproduction.

To begin with, the drawing is no longer the finished article. The printed illustration, advertisement or poster has become in a sense the " original ", and your drawing is just one stage in its production. Between the time when it leaves your hands and the time when you see it again in print, a design goes through a number of complicated processes which may change its appearance quite considerably, in certain respects. You should therefore have in your mind's eye a clear impression of what the final print is to look like, and you must allow in the drawing for modifications which will occur in reproduction. It follows that you must understand the various processes which the engraver can employ. He will, by hook or by crook, reproduce almost anything that is sent to him, but if his task is simplified additional charges will be avoided and the finished article may be more satisfactory. One has, in short, to make concessions to the engraver.

For example: he likes the drawing to be larger than the reproduction required—usually half as large again and never more than twice as large. If a print is to be $4'' \times 5''$ it is usual to make the drawing $6'' \times 7\frac{1}{2}''$. The drawings for the full-page illustrations in this book were $5'' \times 7\frac{3}{4}''$.*

* You will notice that in describing drawings, prints and blocks one always gives the width first and the height second.

Again, all the drawings in a series—drawings made as illustrations to a book, for example—should be to the same scale; they should all require the same reduction.

Line-shading in a drawing made for reproduction should, in view of its intended reduction, be kept rather " open ". Microscopic cross-hatching still further reduced in size will give the engraver a great deal of trouble and will almost certainly print badly. Other restrictions of this kind will be considered in detail later.

Meanwhile it is useful to be able to enlarge or reduce a drawing to any width or height required.

Enlarging and Reducing Drawings.—Figs. 61, 62 and 63 illustrate a method by which this can be done almost mechanically and with great accuracy.

First the drawing is placed squarely in one bottom corner of a larger sheet of paper (Fig. 61). The diagonal AB is drawn and produced, as shown. AC, the width of the enlargement required, is now measured along the bottom of the large sheet of paper and a vertical line is drawn at C until it cuts the diagonal in E. A line draw through E parallel to AC completes a rectangle which has exactly the proportions of the small drawing.

A smaller rectangle can be produced similarly as shown by the dotted line.

Diagonals of the small drawing and of the larger (or smaller) blank sheet are now completed, and lines are drawn through the points of their intersection, parallel to the sides of the rectangles (Fig. 62).

Diagonals are drawn in each of the smaller rectangles formed, and the process is repeated until both sheets are divided into an equal number of compartments—as many as seem necessary.

If you do not wish to spoil the original drawing, this " squaring up " can be done on a piece of tracing paper pinned tightly over it.

You now have a scaffold upon which to construct your new drawing, line by line (Fig. 63). Points chosen in the original can be plotted exactly in the copy by placing them in the corresponding compartment in correct relation with its sides. If it helps, the squares may be numbered.

With practice one can square up a drawing in this way and enlarge it very rapidly.

Photo-process Engraving.—The simplest form of relief printing—wood engraving—was explained in the section of Chapter IX devoted to Scraper Board. It entails cutting away those parts of a block which are required to be white, and leaving in relief, as a printing surface, those which are to be black.

In modern relief printing the principle is exactly the same, but the wood block is replaced by a metal plate, and this is engraved by photographic and chemical processes instead of by hand.

This photo-process engraving is divided into two— line process and half-tone process. The former is used for reproducing originals consisting of jet-black marks on a pure white background; the latter for wash-drawings, photographs, etc., which contain half-tones as well.

These two we must consider in detail. There is a third method, the three-colour process, which enables one to reproduce water-colours, oil paintings, colour photographs, etc., in full colour. It is a development of the half-tone process. You should at a later date learn all you can about this and also about Collotype and Lithography—two other methods by which drawings may be reproduced in black and white.

The Line Process.—A drawing which is to be reproduced by the line process is first of all photographed on to a glass plate. This produces a negative in which all the black parts of the drawing have become transparent and all the white parts black and opaque. If necessary, the opaque parts of the negative can be intensified and the transparent parts cleaned during developing and fixing.

A negative normally comes out backwards, but a prism fixed in front of the lens produces one which appears exactly as the original drawing.

Meanwhile, in a dark room a smooth zinc plate is coated with a substance which is soluble in water but which becomes insoluble if it is exposed to light.

The negative and this sensitised plate are placed together in a printing frame and exposed to electric light for some minutes.

The zinc plate is then removed, covered evenly with a film of sticky ink and held under a tap.

Where the light has penetrated the negative—*i.e.*, in the transparent parts which correspond with the black parts of the drawing—the sensitised coating has become insoluble, and is not affected by the running water.

Where no light has reached the surface, however—*i.e.*, in the opaque parts of the negative, corresponding with the white parts of the drawing—the coating is still soluble and, with the ink which has been rolled on to it, is washed away.

This leaves us with an exact reproduction of the drawing, in reverse, its black parts represented by sticky black ink and its white parts by the smooth, exposed surface of the zinc plate.

A powder called Dragon's Blood is then sprinkled evenly over the plate, sticking to the ink, but not to the smooth zinc, and the whole is heated and rapidly cooled again. This turns the Dragon's Blood into a substance which effectively resists the action of acids.

The surface of the plate is then treated with nitric acid, which etches or eats away the unprotected zinc and leaves the protected parts—the black parts of the drawing—in relief as a printing surface.

The etching process is a very delicate one. It is usually repeated about four times.

The remaining Dragon's Blood is then removed and the whole plate checked, routed, and tooled by hand where necessary.

Finally the plate is nailed to a base of wood or metal —type high—and a proof is " pulled ".

The block is in reverse, but the print will, of course, be the same way round as the original drawing.

Drawing for the Line Process.—Of the media already considered, scraper board and pen and ink (or brush and ink) alone lend themselves to reproduction by the line process.

Pencil, Conté crayon, wash, dry brush and all the other drawings are certain to contain lines and dark passages which are not solid black and which cannot therefore be reproduced by this process.

Half-tones have to be suggested in " line " by arranging for a suitable proportion of white paper to show through the solid black printing ink. In scraper board this is done by ticking or cross-hatching with white lines, while in a pen-and-ink drawing light and shade are built up with black lines, dots, ticks and scribbles (Chapter IX).

In each case the original must be absolutely clear. Ink should always be used neat, without the addition of water.

Some draughtsmen believe that the addition of a little red to their black ink increases its density in reproduction.

Use of as smooth and white and hard a drawing surface as possible also makes for definition and contrast. Bristol Board is excellent.

Chinese white, which is sometimes used for retouching back-and-white drawings, causes a good deal of confusion because it tends to photograph grey. It is as well to avoid it altogether.

Altering a drawing by sticking paper patches over mistakes is another dangerous habit. Under the strong illumination which is used while the drawing is being photographed, the edges of such patches cast small shadows which come out as black lines and have to be cut from the block by hand at a later stage. If a patch must be used it should be as thin and opaque as possible and its edges should be ragged rather than square.

Stray pencil lines left over from the constructional stages of a drawing, dirt and finger-prints may also photograph and come out in the reproduction, so your final cleaning up should be very thorough.

Finally let me commend this line process as a thoroughly satisfactory one. It is the simplest and the least expensive of all, and because the line-block is so akin to type, it is quite the most suitable for book illustration.

The Half-Tone Process.—In all its essentials this is

similar to the line process. A drawing is first of all photographed. Then it is printed on to a sensitised metal plate, and the parts which are to be black are made to resist acid. Finally the unprotected parts are etched away, the plate is mounted type high and the block is complete.

Here, however, a variety of tones can be reproduced—not tones which are suggested by ticking or cross-hatching, but uniform tones such as one produces with a brush and water-colour wash or with a camera.

If you examine a newspaper or magazine illustration or the reproduction of a photograph (*e.g.*, Plate 1 of this book) through a magnifying glass, you will see that it is composed of black dots equidistant but varying in size and shape.

When these are looked at with the naked eye from a suitable distance they fuse with the white paper around or between them, and suggest the even, gradated tones of a photograph or wash-drawing very faithfully.

White is represented by white paper, light tones by very small black dots with a lot of white paper around them, darker tones by larger black dots with less and less white paper between them, and black by solid, unbroken ink. The picture is broken up into these dots mechanically when the original is photographed for reproduction.

A transparent screen, ruled with two sets of parallel, equidistant, diagonal lines, crossing each other at right angles to form an opaque mesh, is placed between the picture and the plate in the camera.

Light reflected from the drawing passes through the mesh (or half-tone screen) in innumerable beams which vary in intensity and which, when they reach the plate, vary also in size.

These produce a negative composed of transparent dots on an opaque background, which in turn produces a zinc or copper half-tone plate composed of dots in relief. This, before a satisfactory print can be taken, may have to be adjusted by hand-etching, dots may have to be reduced in size to improve the light and shade in a print, or be altered in shape to suggest detail more clearly.

The number of lines per square inch in half-tone screens —*i.e.*, in the mesh used for breaking the negative into dots—varies considerably. If prints are to be made on very smooth paper, a very fine mesh may be used, having perhaps 150 or 175 lines to the inch, and a very detailed reproduction will result. For coarser papers a coarser mesh is required. Fifty is usual in newspaper work, and anything up to 150 in magazine illustrations.

The block-maker always knows which screen is best for any particular job, however, so all particulars should be provided and the choice left to him.

Drawing for the Half-Tone Process.—Wash-drawings intended for reproduction are best made with washes of soluble Indian ink diluted with water as required.

Too heavily textured papers produce very coarse prints in both the line and the half-tone processes, but for wash-drawing a slight tooth is necessary. Bristol board is too smooth. White water-colour board is satisfactory in all respects. It should, if anything, incline towards blue. It must not be of the slightly cream variety. A suspicion of red or brown may be introduced into the ink to prevent a bluish tinge appearing in the thinner washes.

Coloured wash-drawings are very uncertain of success in black-and-white reproduction, yellows and blues being particularly dangerous.

Drawings made in body-colour should consist of lamp-black or process black mixed with Chinese white or process white. Process white is preferable to Chinese white because the latter tends to photograph grey and must not, therefore, be used alone.

Wash and body-colour are best not combined in a drawing made for reproduction. They should certainly not be used together until you have had considerable experience of using them separately.

Pencil, Conté pencil, carbon pencil and charcoal drawings all reproduce excellently by this process (see Plates 2 and 3), but scraper-board drawings do not. Passages of solid black and fine black lines, broken into dots, lose contrast with their white background and the whole picture assumes a common greyness. Pen and wash-drawings do not reproduce well by the half-tone process, for the same reason, and a combination of line and half-tone plates may have to be employed. This, naturally, is rather more expensive.

The half-tone process has a levelling effect, even upon wash-drawings and photographs, so the originals of these should always be given a little more contrast than is required in the reproduction.

The half-tone process being more expensive than the line process, numerous attempts have been made to produce, by means of the latter, effects which are normally associated with the former. Textured and patterned scraper boards (Chapter IX) break tones into black dots and lines which can be reproduced by the line process. Greasy litho chalk used on a specially prepared, heavily textured paper produces a similar effect. Unable to reach the hollow parts of the surface, the chalk makes lines and tones which are composed of small, irregular, pure black dots. The rough board does, in fact, the work of the half-tone screen. Examples of this are to be seen in Figs. 20, 32, 37 and 56. The method is not wholly satisfactory, in that the original has all the disadvantages of a drawing made on coarse paper, and because the dots are ragged and lacking in the clear definition which the line process demands.

3. Design.

So much for the technical aspect of drawing for reproduction. The first adjustment which has to be made in actual design is fundamental. It demands a change of attitude.

Representation of Colour.—So far you have been given to understand that drawing is concerned with form alone, and not with colour. That is true when you are making a " pure " drawing, but illustrations, posters and advertisements are not necessarily pure drawings. One has frequently to suggest in black and white the different colours of objects as well as the gradations of light and shade upon them. It may be necessary, for example, to show patterns on clothes or curtains which differ from their backgrounds only in colour; it may be necessary to differentiate in black and white between a fair man and a dark one—between a white man and a negro.

Pattern and the Decorative Idea.—Secondly, lettering, which plays a great part in commercial and industrial work, is essentially two dimensional; and for this reason, if for no other, one is compelled to think in terms of shape more often than in terms of space—in flat patterns rather than in forms.

An illustration is a picture having a bearing upon the text of a book, but it must also be—and this is really

FIG. 64.

more important—a pattern which decorates the page and harmonises with adjacent type. Too great a sense of depth and solidity in an illustration may well destroy rather than decorate the surface of a page. It is better to produce something which is frankly flat and decorative; a pattern of shapes; of small richly textured passages and larger less detailed areas; of fine arabesques balanced by steady, solid masses.

A page of type and illustration, a poster, a showcard or, for that matter, any drawing or painting, turned upside down, and so stripped of all literary meaning, should continue to please the eye with its texture, pattern, light and shade. It should in short, have an abstract beauty quite distinct from the beauty of places, people and incidents depicted.

This principle, possibly because photography has exerted so strong an influence on the average artist, is often completely lost sight of in contemporary work.

Drawings reproduced by the line process have a great deal in common with type, and a degree of harmony between them is inevitable. Wood engravings and scraper-board drawings are, for this reason, particularly suitable for book illustration.

Distortion.—Certain distortions of truth are sometimes permissible if they improve the drawing as a design. For example, cast shadows rendered in their full tonal values tend to destroy the balance of a pattern, so, in illustrations, decorative panels and mural paintings they are often reduced to the very palest greys, or are left out altogether. Perspective, too, can sometimes be usefully wangled in the construction of a design, while proportion, particularly in the human figure, is frequently distorted. The two last expedients should be resorted to only by the very experienced draughtsman.

The mediaeval painter and illustrator was a master of distortion in design, but in his work it usually has great literary significance as well. Children's paintings exhibit strangely similar features. Deeply concerned with the meaning of a subject rather than with its presentation, they make the more important figures—the bride and bridegroom at a wedding, for example—much larger than their fellows; larger even than trees and buildings.

Heads of people and animals in modern drawings are often made smaller than is natural, in order to accentuate the size and strength of the body. This may be done quite unconsciously. It was, at one time, a popular convention in paintings of prize cattle and horses.

Commercial Work—Beginning.—First excursions into this new kind of work should be based on your early model drawings. Take a number of them and adjust them from the point of view of design until they fulfil the conditions of a number of hypothetical commissions.

A layout pad costing about two shillings, made of almost transparent paper, will be of assistance here. A drawing made on one sheet can be traced on to the next, and from that on to the next, being gradually altered and pulled together until a satisfactory arrangement is arrived at.

Borrow or buy a book of alphabets and introduce a few words in Roman or Sans Serif capitals. Remember that the drawing and the lettering are both parts of the same pattern, and design them together.

Solid-looking drawings of cardboard houses plus a little lettering will advertise a new Housing Estate or the wares of an imaginary builder's merchant; cubes and cylinders can be converted quite easily into loaves of bread and tins of fruit on catalogue covers or in posters. More advanced drawing groups, consisting of shoes, fabrics, cups and saucers, etc., will, with a little suggested colour, provide further subjects.

Then translate these ideas into media suitable for reproduction by the line and half-tone processes. First try to express them in quite broad masses of black and white. Then do them again introducing textures, showing the form of all objects involved and suggesting their colour as well where necessary.

Finally make pen-and-ink, scraper-board and wash-drawings of your chosen subjects along the lines already indicated in this chapter and in Chapter IX.

Make some drawings for Chrismas cards and calendars. These have to be decorative to the exclusion of all else (Fig. 64).

Book Illustration.—Later you should take a short book and make a series of illustrations, larger than the intended reproductions and in a suitable medium.

Select one which is congenial to you. It might be an adventure, a travel book or a fairy story. Children's books are popular subjects among illustrators nowadays, particularly perhaps among girl students. They allow great freedom of treatment and can be very decorative.

If you make illustrations for a new book you will be very unlikely to sell them. Illustrations are usually commissioned by a publisher and appear in an early edition of a book. Later and cheaper editions are not as a rule illustrated with a new set of drawings. If you hope to sell your drawings it is safer to choose an old and well-established favourite which a publisher might be tempted to reprint with illustrations.

All that has been written about composition and arrangement of trees, figures, etc., in pictures, applies equally in illustrations.

Your reference file should, of course, be invaluable here.

Possible illustrations and decorations for a book are as follows :

A frontispiece. The use of this is a convention which is gradually falling out of use.

Full-page illustrations.

Double spreads or double-page illustrations.

Drawings in the text—*i.e.*, small drawings set in among the type.

Chapter headings.

Tail-pieces.

This book gives you examples of most of these, but variations of them are legion.

You are shown also, in this book, several ways of finishing an illustration. Figs. 2, 3, 4, 10, 11, 12, etc., have a single black line border. Figs. 5, 6 and 7 show variations of this. Figs. 9 and 57 have borders consisting of parallel lines of varying thickness, while Plates 1 and 2 and Figs. 41, 48, 58 and 60 have no borders at all.

In many modern books the illustrations, both drawn and photographic, are taken right to the edge of the page, leaving no margin.

Book Jackets.—The paper dust-cover on a good modern book is designed with as much care as the illustrations inside.

It is usually in colour, but pen-and-ink, pen-and-wash, wash-drawings and body-colour are quite suitable.

The design generally covers the front and the spine of the book, but sometimes the back is included as well. Often one continuous drawing can be folded right round the book, but parts of the design which coincide with the front, back and spine, and which may therefore be seen separately, must each be complete in itself.

Alternatively, the jacket can be designed in separate panels.

The lettering and the drawing in such designs should be so arranged that both contribute to the total effect. One should never feel that the lettering might be removed without detriment to the whole.

Magazine Illustration.—Possibilities here are much the same as in book illustration. Double spreads, chapter headings, tail-pieces, etc., are used in the same way, but greater liberties are taken with them.

A magazine is a less permanent thing than a book; it is an incident and, as such, it needs to be more novel, more arresting.

You will see, by looking in any copy of one of the better-class weekly or monthly publications, the type of work which is required and what forms it can take.

Keep good illustrations from such magazines in the appropriate section of your reference file.

Have a section there, too, for any interesting alphabets, or parts of alphabets which you may collect. One is often in need of a suitable piece of drawn lettering.

Finally, when designing posters, book-jackets, book or magazine illustrations, you must avoid conscious striving after originality. Concentrate always on quality, and be as sincere as you can. If you have an innate style it will appear in your work quite naturally.

4. Mounts.

The young artist peddling his work round the offices of agents and publishers has a lot to learn from the commercial traveller. He must know how to make his wares attractive; that is the greater part of the art of salesmanship.

Presented with ragged edges, in a pile of limp sheets

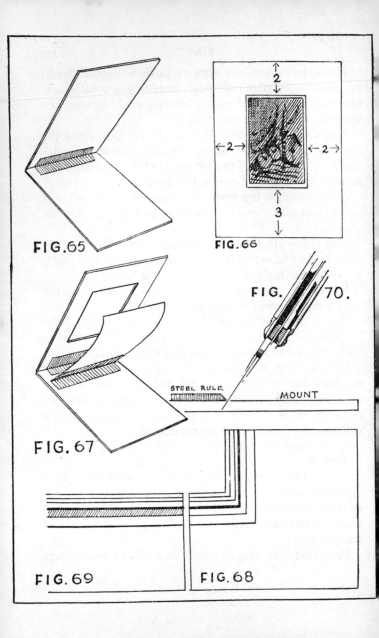

FIG. 65

FIG. 66

FIG. 67

FIG. 70.

STEEL RULE.

MOUNT

FIG. 69

FIG. 68

all shapes and sizes, first-class drawings may receive no more than a cursory glance. Some may be completely overlooked.

Carefully mounted between stiff cards they are easily handled, none are likely to be missed and all are certain to receive more attention. Drawings look their best in the splendid isolation afforded by a broad, light-coloured mount.

Figs. 65 to 70 illustrate the best method of mounting drawings. Two cards of the same size and shape considerably larger than the drawing, and of a suitable proportion, are selected. Heavy plate paper is excellent for this purpose, but any hard, thin card will do. A tinted surface may be used if desired.

These two cards are then hinged inside at the top with a strip of gummed paper (Fig. 65).

Next a rectangle is marked out on the front card, equidistant from top and sides and about half as far again from the bottom edge. It should be between a quarter and half an inch wider than the drawing and about three-quarters of an inch deeper (Fig. 66).

If your drawing goes right to the edge of its paper, at least one-eighth of an inch of all edges will have to be hidden by the mount. The rectangle should therefore be made that much smaller than the drawing.

You will learn from experience the proportions most satisfactory in the margins of mounts and drawings of various sizes.

The rectangle is now cut out with a sharp knife, used along a steel ruler. The corners must be cut very clean and square.

The drawing can now be hinged on to the back board

with gummed paper or pasted on to it by the top corners (Fig. 67).

When the mount is closed, the drawing must appear squarely in the cut-out rectangle, its top and side margins equal and the bottom margin slightly deeper (Fig. 66).

For drawings which are to be submitted to an agent or a studio, mounts should be quite plain, but when a drawing is to be framed, perhaps for exhibition, a series of parallel lines unevenly spaced and of varying thickness may be used a little way from the edges of the aperture (Fig. 68).

These should be made in black or sepia ink or in pencil, and the space between two of them may sometimes be effectively filled with a wash of pale grey, green or brown water-colour (Fig. 69).

When a thick mount is used, its appearance will be improved if you bevel the edges of the aperture.   This is done by holding your knife against and under the edge of the steel rule at an angle of 45 degrees, the point directed away from the edge of the board.   Fig. 70 shows a back view of the knife and the rule when this bevelling is in progress.

You will find that it is economical to use plate paper or good quality board for the front of the mount only. Strawboard or anything stiff and strong may be used for the back.

5. Placing Work.

When, from among the masses of drawings you produce, you can select ten or a dozen which are really good, mount them carefully and put them away in a portfolio.

Reconsider them at a later date, and if in the light of greater experience some of them seem now to be technically unsound or badly designed, remove them and replace them by more recent and more competent efforts.

Very gradually you will build up, in this way, a small but representative collection of work.

You are not likely to find purchasers for these drawings, but if they are attractive they may encourage firms and agents to commission other work. Posters for an imaginary vacuum cleaner may persuade a real manufacturer that you are just the man to publicise some very different product.

The usual approach to such possible customers is through an agent—the accepted go-between.

The first few agents you call upon may see at a glance that the type of work you are submitting will not attract their clients, and you must not therefore be disappointed if they show no interest. Look farther afield until you encounter one who thinks that he will be able to find a use for you.

This last agent may borrow your portfolio of drawings and take them round a number of firms. One of these may be tempted to see how your work will appeal to his public and you are handed the details of a small job.

It is now for you to make this first commission a real success. If it goes down well the agent will almost certainly find you more work, and with this fact as a lever you may persuade other agents to take you up as well.

Some draughtsmen are fortunate in producing work which appeals to a very large public. The agent has no difficulty in finding commissions for such as these, for he is able to pass almost any problem to them and be reasonably sure of an attractive and popular solution.

Other artists—a little highbrow, perhaps—work for a more limited public, and may therefore receive commissions only on rare occasions; they may even have difficulty in finding an agent who can place their work.

A great many artists approach firms direct, particularly if those firms are known to have advanced ideas and a taste for spotting new talent themselves. There is no harm in this, and one should do it whenever occasion arises. The advantages of working through an agent are, however, obvious. By saving all the time which is wasted trekking round offices and waiting for interviews, he enables one to spend a full-working day or evening (if that is all one can spare) in the studio, and so to produce considerably more work. In return, he deducts a quite reasonable percentage from the price paid for each job.

I intended dealing with this business of marketing in some detail, but at the time of writing matters artistic are greatly disorganised, and it is impossible to say whether they will ever reassume exactly their pre-war form.

In any case we are looking rather far ahead. It is by no accident that the selling of work has been left to the end of this book—it is usually the last thing one is able to do, and it is also the last thing one should bother about. You must certainly learn to walk before you attempt to run.

Your first chances of doing actual jobs will probably be found in your own neighbourhood. They may well be voluntary and unpaid—work for Bazaars, Amateur

Dramatic Shows, Dances, etc.—but they should all be done as well as you know how to do them.   Never scamp a piece of work, however unremunerative it may be.

Bad publicity is fatal.   Nothing less than your very best should ever leave your hands.

Good publicity may lead, however, to paid commissions from local firms and very valuable practice under real working conditions.

Reproductions of such work will also look well among the drawings with which you do, finally, invade the agents.